SCHOOL HANDBOOKS: LEGAL CONSIDERATIONS

Second Edition

by
Mary Angela Shaughnessy, SCN, J.D., Ph.D.

Department of Elementary Schools
National Catholic Educational Association

Copyright 2002
National Catholic Educational Association
1077 30th Street, NW, Suite 100
Washington, D.C.   20007-3852
ISBN #1-55833-281-2

Second Printing 2004

a. m. Showers

TABLE OF CONTENTS

DEDICATION

I dedicate this work to the memory of
a man who dedicated his life to social change,
a man who worked tirelessly to fight discrimination,
a man who sought to better the working conditions of minorities,
a man who led union pickets,
a man who marched in Selma, Alabama,
a man who believed each person has a responsibility to challenge
    injustice,
a man who was my uncle,
Harry Bartlett Shaughnessy,
on the nineteenth anniversary of his death.

Harry Bartlett Shaughnessy
1917-1983

ACKNOWLEDGEMENTS

Thirteen years have passed since the publication of my text, *School Handbooks: Legal Considerations for the Administrator.* Today's educators face challenges that once were unthinkable. This text attempts to address the issues that should be considered in handbook development. Many people have walked the last thirteen years with me, and I am grateful. I express special gratitude to the many who have studied with me and who have generously shared their insights. Without them, the writing of such a text would be much more difficult.

I wish to express special gratitude to Dr. Robert Kealey, Executive Director of the National Catholic Education Association, who was willing to take a chance on a relative unknown and publish that first edition of *School Handbooks* in 1989. Bob is retiring this year and takes with him the gratitude of those who minister in Catholic education.

I also wish to thank my boss, Dr. Thomas Oates, President of Spalding University, who has patiently allowed me to travel the country giving workshops and teaching classes. His support of my research is most appreciated.

I thank my family, especially the next generation, whose years in Catholic schools continue to provide me with inspiration for my writing. I thank my religious community, the Sisters of Charity of Nazareth, who support my ministry.

Finally, I thank you, the reader. May this text make a small contribution to your educational ministry in the Catholic Church.

Mary Angela Shaughnessy, SCN, J.D., Ph.D.

PREFACE

Thirteen years ago, NCEA first published a book on school handbooks entitled *School Handbooks: Some Legal Considerations* by Sister Mary Angela Shaughnessy, SCN, J.D., Ph.D. During that time, this book has gone through five printings and thousands of copies of it have been purchased by principals, pastors, school board members and other Catholic educators. It has been the accepted textbook in many graduate classes on school law for Catholic school educators. While the basic principles of law have not changed during this period, the world is a very different place than it was in 1989. Therefore, a revision is needed.

Handbooks for students, parents and faculty are very important documents. In them the school indicates what responsibilities the student, parent or faculty member has toward the school. The handbooks also acknowledge the responsibilities that the school has toward the student, parent or faculty member. School handbooks serve almost like a contract among students, parents, faculty and school administrators.

Various courts across the nation have examined school handbooks and rendered decisions based upon what is contained in them. Therefore, school administrators must take great pains to ensure that what is written in their school handbooks is absolutely correct. The obligations placed on the student, parent or faculty member are reasonable and the specifications outlined for the school can be achieved. Finally, the school administrator must ensure that on a day to day basis the requirements set forth in the handbooks are being fulfilled.

Sister Mary Angela Shaughnessy has provided invaluable help to NCEA and its membership throughout these years by her writings and her presentations at NCEA Conventions and diocesan meetings. The NCEA Department of Elementary Schools expresses its gratitude to Sister Angela for completely revising her previous work. Hundreds of hours of research, thought, and writing have gone into producing this new book. Once again Sister Angela has provided for the Catholic school community a complete and easy to use text that will be on the desks of thousands of Catholic educators for many years to come.

The NCEA Department of Elementary Schools offers this publication to its members with the hope that they will find it helpful in their ministry of education. It also believes that by following the advice provided in this work the members will be assisted in providing wise counsel to students, teachers and parents.

The NCEA Department of Elementary Schools thanks Janice Kraus, editorial assistant in the department, for her help in seeing this publication through its production process. It expresses its gratitude to Beatriz Ruiz for her work in designing the cover and formatting the pages.

Janet P. Murray, M.A.　　　　　*Robert J. Kealey, Ed.D.*
President　　　　　　　　　*Executive Director*

Department of Elementary Schools
National Catholic Educational Association
Feast of St. Katherine Drexel 2002

ABOUT THE AUTHOR

Sister Mary Angela Shaughnessy, SCN, J.D., Ph.D., is a Sister of Charity of Nazareth who has taught at all levels of Catholic education from elementary through graduate school. She served eight years as principal of a Catholic high school. Sister Mary Angela holds a bachelor's degree in English, a master's degree in English, a master's degree in educational administration, a J.D. in Law and a Ph.D. in Educational Administration and Supervision. Her research centers on the law as it affects Catholic education and Church ministry. She is the author of over twenty books.

A consultant to numerous dioceses, Sister Mary Angela is a regular speaker at the NCEA conventions. Sister has served as an adjunct professor in various college and university programs. She has served as visiting professor at the University of San Francisco since 1988. Sister has served on several White House committees through the United States Department of Education. Currently, Sister Mary Angela is general legal counsel and Professor of Education at Spalding University in Louisville, Kentucky. She is a member of the bar in the state of Kentucky.

Sister is the recipient of numerous awards, including the NCEA Secondary Department Award and the D'Amour/O'Neill Award for Outstanding Service to Boards of Catholic Education. In 1977, she was named one of the twenty-five most influential persons in Catholic education over the past twenty-five years.

INTRODUCTION

The lived reality of the third millennium is certainly different from that of the 1990s. Americans struggle with safety and security issues not previously known or contemplated. Yet, parents and students expect school administrators and personnel to ensure student safety. School administrators, familiar with ever-increasing numbers of lawsuits, know that legally sound handbooks provide the best protection from costly litigation and judgments. Painfully aware that there are no absolute safety guarantees, administrators seek to develop and implement operational policies and procedures that will help their school communities achieve two most important goals: the promotion of education and the protection of children.

In the introduction to the 1989 NCEA text, *School Handbooks*, this author wrote, "One of the more formidable tasks facing any Catholic school administrator is that of developing and writing school handbooks, those definitive references containing policies and procedures for which school community members are responsible." In the light of the recent past decade or so, the task is perhaps even more formidable. Many an administrator has reflected on earlier days when school administration seemed simpler and the tasks more achievable. Today's students, no less than yesterday's, deserve the best efforts of teachers and administrators. Handbooks are instruments that aid all members of the school community in the realization of the school's mission and ministry.

In this era of accountability, educators know only too well that they are accountable to many entities. State educational authorities regulate Catholic and other private schools through statutes and regulations. Administrators in Catholic schools must also answer to pastors in parish schools, to governing bodies of religious congregations, to governing and advisory boards, and to diocesan officials. Administrators are accountable to parents for the education their children receive and for the competence of the school personnel providing those experiences. Administrators are expected to give faculty and staff clear directions and to provide personnel policies that are just. Catholic school administrators must be concerned not only with legality, but also with the morality of their actions.

Catholic school administrators have much wider latitude in developing rules than do their public school counterparts because students, teachers and parents in Catholic schools cannot claim the guarantees of the United States Constitution while in Catholic schools, since the Constitution only governs what public officials do. A public school is a public institution and those who govern it are public officials. Catholic schools are private institutions governed by private individuals; thus, contract and other statutory law, not Constitutional law, will apply. Although civil law is not the same in the public and private sectors, Catholic school administrators need an understanding of the evolution of law in the public school sector. Court decisions can offer guidance for Catholic school administrators seeking to develop legally sound and morally just policies and procedures. A brief mention of early significant public sector cases is in order.

The last forty years have witnessed a dramatic increase in the numbers and kinds of lawsuits brought against schools in general. Prior to the 1960s, only a small number of cases involving parents, students and/or teachers resulted in findings against schools. Judges, practicing the doctrine of judicial restraint, which required judges to refrain from interfering in decisions made by competent professionals unless the decision "shocked the court," tended to rule in favor of the schools in such disputes. While the doctrine of judicial restraint is still applicable, judges seem to be somewhat more willing today than in the past to decide against schools, particularly in the area of student discipline. At the same time, hard won public school student freedoms are not always upheld. Safety concerns have more recently led to judicial decisions upholding requiring students to wear uniforms in public schools, a decision that would have been unthinkable only a decade ago.

The History of Student Rights

A landmark college case set the stage for many education cases in 1961. In *Dixon v. Alabama State Board of Education* 294 F.2d 150, *cert. den.* 368 U.S. 930, students in a public university were suspended for participating in a lunch counter sit-in. The justices ruled that students in public colleges and universities had the right to procedural due process. College administrators could no longer arbitrarily dismiss students or teachers at will. The accused had to be given a minimum of due process: *notice*, the person is told what it is he or she is alleged to have done; *hearing*, the person is given an opportunity to present his or her side of the story; *before an impartial tribunal* (and judges will assume, in the absence of evidence to the contrary, that a school official is an impartial party.) Thus the court reasoned that education in a state university is a property interest. The court did not require a full-scale hearing for the students, but it did require that the basic elements of due process be met. Later decisions would require that a full panoply of due process protections, nine in all, be afforded students facing serious disruption of their education. Although Catholic schools are not required to grant Constitutional due process, they are held to standards of fairness which generally require the same three minimum elements of Constitutional due process, not because of the Constitution, but because of the requirements of good faith and fair dealing, how reasonable persons can be expected to treat each other.

After the *Dixon* case, many elementary and secondary cases were litigated. Three of these have particular historic significance. *Tinker v. Des Moines Independent Community School District et al.* 393 U.S. 503 (1969) produced the now famous statement, "It can hardly be argued that either students or teachers shed their constitutional rights to freedom of speech or expression at the [public] schoolhouse gate" (p. 506). Although this case involving students who were suspended from public elementary and secondary schools for wearing black armbands to protest the Vietnam War is rightfully associated with First Amendment freedom of speech rights, it is very significant in Fourteenth Amendment due process considerations as well. In the public sector, First Amendment rights cannot be restricted without due process of law.

A second landmark public school case, *Goss v. Lopez* 419 U.S. 565 (1974), involved Ohio public school students who had been suspended from school for up to ten days without a hearing. The United States Supreme Court ruled that suspended public school students do have rights to at least minimal due process protections. The *Goss* court called for actions based on a moral viewpoint, a sense of fair play, as much as on what the Constitution does and does not require. Courts rely on an expectation that educators are trying to do the right and honorable thing. Since educators are supposed to be modeling appropriate behaviors for students, courts will hold educators to strict standards of "fair play" where student misconduct is alleged. In a second case heard the same day as *Goss*, i.e., *Wood v. Strickland*, 420 U.S. 308 (1974), the court ruled that public school officials could be held liable for damages if their actions violated the rights of students. By 1974, then, the rights of public school students and teachers appeared to be firmly established.

Catholic and other private schools, like public schools, are expected to be fair in their dealings with students and teachers, but that fairness is judged by the provisions of the contract existing between the school and the student or teacher, rather than by Constitutional issues. No Constitutional due process protections exist in Catholic schools. Because the Catholic school is not an extension of the state, students and teachers cannot generally claim Constitutional protections. This lack of Constitutional safeguards does not mean that Catholic schools may be arbitrary in their dealings with parents, students and teachers, but it does mean that Catholic educators do not have to accept all the behaviors that the public school has no choice but to accept. The last twenty-five years or so have witnessed a rise in the number of cases brought by Catholic school students, parents and teachers. The reticence that once seemed to keep a church member from suing a church authority has largely disappeared. Previously, the doctrine of separation of church and state protected church-sponsored schools from being successfully sued. More recent decisions suggest that the doctrine does not offer a church-related institution absolute protection from successful lawsuits.

Case law in private schools is growing. Although the United States Supreme Court has heard only one private school teacher dismissal case, *Rendell-Baker v. Kohn 102* S.Ct. 2764 and that decision was reached in 1982, there is indication that courts are more willing to hear private school cases than they were in the past.

In 1990 Catholic school administrators were largely unconcerned with students bringing guns to schools. When shootings occurred in public schools, some thought such events would never happen in Catholic schools. But shootings and other violence have occurred in Catholic schools and it is only to be expected that when persons are injured in institutions, those who administer the institutions will be sued.

The study of civil law as it impacts Catholic schools is no longer new. The law is in a state of constant development and administrators of Catholic schools must be knowledgeable about the rights of persons in their institutions and their own responsibilities to protect those rights.

Catholic school administrators, concerned with both the duty to act justly and with the avoidance of litigation, are wise to seek guidance in the writing of documents, especially handbooks. This text provides an introduction to the laws affecting the administration of Catholic schools and offers specific guidance concerning the contents and wording of faculty, parent/student and board handbooks.

Administrators may be discouraged when confronted with the writing of handbooks in addition to the already demanding tasks of school administration; however, well-written, legally sound handbooks can do much to ensure the smooth operation of Catholic schools.

CHAPTER ONE—
CATHOLIC EDUCATION
AND CIVIL LAW

This chapter will discuss how civil law applies to situations in Catholic schools. While certainly not exhaustive, it is intended to be a good introduction for those who do not have a background in the topic and a comprehensive review for those who do. Knowledge of school law is a prerequisite for handbook development.

Sources of the Law

Laws governing schools in the United States generally fall into one of four categories: (1) constitutional law (both state and federal); (2) administrative law, consisting of statutes and regulations; (3) common law principles; and (4) contract law. Public school law and private school law can differ greatly, as the following discussion will illustrate.

Constitutional law

Federal Constitutional law guarantees that government will not arbitrarily deprive individuals of their Constitutional freedoms. Constitutional law protects students and teachers in public schools since public schools are government agencies administered by government officials. Federal Constitutional law does not protect students and teachers in non-public schools because private schools are private agencies. When a student enrolls in a Catholic school, a private institution, he or she does not have

Constitutional protections while in that Catholic school. Of course, a person in a Catholic school can always voluntarily leave that institution and enter the public sector where Constitutional rights are protected, but so long as the person remains in the private, Catholic sector, the Constitution offers no protection.

Therefore, what cannot lawfully be done in a public school may be done in a Catholic school. For example, the First Amendment to the Constitution protects persons' rights to free speech; therefore, administrators in public schools may not make rules prohibiting the expression of an unpopular viewpoint, unless the expression constitutes a clear danger to safety. Since no such Constitutional protection exists in the Catholic school, administrators may restrict the speech of both students and teachers. One example of such restriction is the prohibition of supporting a position that violates the teaching of the Catholic Church. A teacher is not free to state that the Church is wrong in a certain teaching, even if the individual sincerely believes that the Church is wrong. School employees are agents of the Catholic Church and are expected to "hold the company line." The first legal obligation of the Catholic school and its employees is to provide a *Catholic* education (emphasis on Catholic). Sometimes, this reality is painful. The Church does not claim to be perfect, but persons who are responsible for the Catholic education of young persons must be careful to live a life consistent with the teachings of the Catholic Church.

State Action

The only time a Catholic school will be required to grant federal Constitutional protections is if state action can be found to be so pervasive within a given school action that school officials can fairly be said to be acting as agents of the state. State action can be defined as:

> In general, [a] term used in connection with claims under due process clause and Civil Rights Act for which a private citizen is seeking damages or redress because of improper

governmental intrusion into his life. In determining whether an action complained of constitutes "state action" within purview of the Fourteenth Amendment, court must determine whether sufficiently close nexus exists between state and challenged action so that the action may fairly be treated as that of the state itself. (Black, p.1407).

Therefore, if state action can be demonstrated to exist in an institution or in a specific program or activity of an institution, Constitutional protections, of which due process is one, must be provided. To date, no court of record has found state action present in a private school to such an extent that Constitutional protections are triggered. In the previously cited *Rendell-Baker v. Kohn* case, the court declined to find state action even though the school received as much as 99% of its operating funds from the state.

In the landmark 1925 case of *Pierce v. the Society of Sisters* 268 U.S. 510, the United States Supreme Court ruled that private schools have the right to exist. The state of Oregon had passed a law, which would have required parents to send all children between the ages of eight and sixteen to public schools. The enforcement of the law would have closed Catholic and other private schools. The court ruled that such a law was unconstitutional. The court also observed that the statute unreasonably interfered with the rights of parents to choose the education of their children. Thus, the right of parents to choose their children's schools was firmly established.

Given then that Catholic schools have a right to exist and since they are not bound to grant Constitutional protections, litigants alleging a denial of Constitutional rights will have to prove the existence of significant state action within the institution before the court will grant relief. Catholic school administrators and teachers must understand that it is contract and statutory law, not the Constitution, which governs Catholic schools. It is not uncommon for parents, students or teachers to claim that their federal Constitutional rights have been violated in the Catholic school when, in fact, no Constitutional rights ever existed.

Some of the main arguments advanced to prove the presence of state action in private schools are: (1) an institution's acceptance of government monies; (2) the tax-exempt status of the school; (3) education as a quasi-state function, sometimes called a "public benefit theory" since schools perform a public service; and (4) state involvement with the school through accreditation or similar procedures and/or statutory requirements with which the school complies.

A 1970 Indiana case, *Bright v. Isenbarger* 314 F.Supp. 1382, is one of the earliest Catholic school discipline cases. Two high school sophomores were suspended from a Catholic school for violation of a school rule. The dismissed students alleged state action in: state regulation of educational standards; tax-exempt status of the school; school receipt of federal and state aid. The court rejected the arguments and found no significant state action. Further, the court ruled that even if significant state action had been found, it would have to be substantially involved in the contested activity, the expulsion, for Constitutional protections to have been triggered. The court concluded:

> Not only do plaintiffs fail to have any compelling judicial support for their contentions but they have invited this court to adopt a rationale of decision which would effectively eliminate private education. . . . A decision which would encompass such a result raises questions of profound Constitutional significance, since the right of parents to maintain and of children to attend private schools is among their fundamental personal liberties and enriches our highly valued tradition of social pluralism. . . . Yet the fact that the State provides tuition-free schools in order to promote an educated citizenry does not mean that *all private* educational institutions perform a "public function." (pp. 1397-98).

The *Bright* court definitely rejected the "public benefit" theory as it applies to the Catholic school. One cannot conclude that Catholic schools perform a public function because they perform a public service.

In a second significant case, *Geraci v. St. Xavier High School* Ohio Opinions 13 3d 146 (1978), a student who had been expelled for encouraging someone to throw a pie in the face of a teacher during a final exam, invoked the state action argument. The court sought to determine whether a "symbiotic relationship" existed between the state and the administration and operation of the school to such an extent that state action could be proven to exist. Earlier public school decisions clearly stated that public education was a right extended by the state, and, therefore, state action is present in the conduct of public school officials; in *Geraci*, the court had to determine whether state action could possibly be construed as being present in any of the school's operations. The court did not find a symbiotic relationship, or any other type of state action present in the school and ruled that private schools are not bound by due process considerations as required by the federal Constitution. However, the court did indicate that courts could intervene in the disciplinary proceedings of private schools and cautioned that private school administrators were not free to do anything they wished:

> A private school's disciplinary proceedings are not controlled by the due process clause, and accordingly such schools have broad discretion in making rules and setting up procedures for their enforcement, nevertheless, under its broad equitable powers a court will intervene where such discretion is abused or the proceedings do not comport with fundamental fairness. (pp. 149-50)

This court suggests that, even if state action does not exist in private schools, the schools may still be held to a standard of "fundamental fairness." This phrase is sometimes used as a synonym for due process, although *Constitutional* due process requires specific protections as laid down in law and interpreted by courts. Fundamental reasonableness and commonly accepted standards of fair play govern the operation of Catholic schools.

These early private school cases and more recent ones indicate that courts will not hold Catholic school administrators to the requirements of the Constitution, but to a lesser standard based on how reasonable people should be expected to treat each other.

In any consideration of fairness in the private sector, some discussion of due process in the public sector is in order. Almost all cases concerning student and teacher rights in public schools involve the legal concept of due process. Although Constitutional due process is not required in Catholic schools, administrators may find knowledge of due process and its implications helpful in the development and implementation of rules, procedures and policies. Some historical background concerning due process is necessary if administrators are to develop policies which are legally and morally defensible.

Due Process

The democratic principle of due process on which Constitutional due process is based is rooted in the theory of the social contract first articulated by the philosopher Plato and developed in more modern times by Locke and Rousseau: "The justification for the state's existence according to Locke, was based on its ability to protect those rights better than individuals could on their own" (LaMorte, p. 32). Locke's ideas are reflected in the Declaration of Independence which guarantees "certain inalienable rights, among these are life, liberty and the pursuit of happiness." The Fifth Amendment to the Constitution guarantees that no person shall "be deprived of life, liberty or property, without due process of law." The Fourteenth Amendment extends that guarantee to the actions of individual states and protects the citizen from arbitrary state action: "No state shall make or enforce any law which shall abridge the privileges or immunities of the citizens of the United Sates; nor shall any State deprive any person of life, liberty or property, without due process of law." These Amendments provide the basis for due process arguments in public school settings.

The Civil Rights Act of 1871 protects persons whose individual Constitutional rights are denied by state authorities. The Civil Rights Act applies to persons acting—or upon the receiving end of actions "under color of state law." The actions of private individuals who are not agents of the state are not governed by the Civil Rights Act or by the Constitution. Therefore, Catholic school administrators generally cannot be legally required to provide Constitutional due process protections, unless such protections are guaranteed by contract. Catholic school administrators should not give students Constitutional due process rights in handbooks or regulations unless they intend to honor all Constitutional freedoms. Nonetheless, Catholic school administrators should develop and act upon a Christian due process model which, while not Constitutional, is one that protects the right of individuals in the light of the Gospel and Church documents.

Procedural due process has been defined with questions: what process is due? What procedures are followed? Are they reasonable? Are all persons treated fairly and, insofar as possible, in the same way? Are there clear procedures that persons can expect will be followed?

Traditionally, courts have held that there are two types of due process: procedural and substantive. The concept of substantive due process is somewhat more difficult to understand than is the concept of procedural due process. Its root word, *substance*, might be helpful in understanding the concept. A person cannot violate someone's substantive due process rights unless the "substance" of which one is to be deprived is one to which the individual has an existing right. Substantive due process involves moral as well as legal ramifications: is this action fair and reasonable? Substantive due process applies whenever *property* or *liberty* interests can be shown.

Property interest has been defined as "everything which is or may be the subject of ownership, whether [it is] a legal ownership . . .or a private ownership." (Black, p. 1216) A person's tangible property constitutes a property interest. In the public sector, the right to an education in public schools is a property interest guaranteed by the state. But certain conditions must be met before a property interest, such as tenure, can be advanced.

Teachers in Catholic schools who have tenure have a contractual, rather than a Constitutional, property interest. Catholic schools do not always have written policies regarding tenure. Most dioceses and parishes maintain that everyone is on a year-to-year contract and no one is guaranteed contract renewal. Thus, a Catholic school administrator may decline to renew the one year contract of a teacher employed for twenty-five years in the school and a court may very well uphold the non-renewal.

A liberty interest concerns a person's right to freedom and reputation. In a Catholic school, questions regarding the morality and fairness of proposed actions should be given at least as much attention as legal ones. It would seem that the Judaeo/Christian ethic requires that at least the rudiments of due process be offered persons in Catholic schools. Granting a minimum of Christian due process would not only meet Gospel demands, but would also help to ensure that Catholic school officials are acting in wise and ethical ways.

Administrative Law: Statutes and Regulations

Administrative law, which encompasses federal and state statutes and regulations, governs the public school and, in many instances, may govern the private school as well. Failure to comply with reasonable regulations can result in the imposition of sanctions. The 1983 case, *Bob Jones University v. United States* 103 S.Ct. 2017 illustrates this point. When Bob Jones University, a private religious school, was found to use racially discriminatory admissions and discipline policies, the Internal Revenue Service withdrew the university's tax-exempt status based on a 1970 regulation proscribing the granting of tax-exempt status to any institution which discriminated on the basis of race. Before a religious school will be penalized for non-compliance with a law or regulation, the state will have to demonstrate a *compelling interest* in its enforcement. Black defines compelling state interest as; "[t]erm used to uphold state action in the face of attack, grounded on Equal Protection or First Amendment rights because of serious need for such state action." (p. 282). In the *Bob Jones* case, the government's compelling interest in racial equality was sufficient for the court to order the university to comply with the anti-discrimination regulation or lose its tax-exempt status. Religious schools must abide by discrimination law; the one exception lies in religious discrimination. Catholic schools may give preference in admissions and hiring to Catholics.

The law of negligence is a type of statutory law. Because the theory of legal negligence affects virtually every aspect of school operations, the next chapter is devoted to a discussion of negligence.

Common law

The third type of law, which applies to both public and private schools, is common law. Common law consists of previous court decisions that have not been overruled by more recent decisions. Sometimes called judge-made law, common law principles may also be considered to be derived from God's law. Many common law principles are rooted in basic morality, such as that found in the Bible. Therefore, it is not uncommon for a court to discuss basic fairness or common law standards of decency in a decision, even without reference to specific state or federal law.

Contract Law

The fourth type of law governing both public and private schools is contract law. Contract law, especially in the area of teacher employment can govern public schools. Most cases involving public schools allege violation of Constitutionally protected interests, which triggers a greater degree of protection than mere contract violation. In the Catholic school, contract law is the predominant governing law. A contract may be defined as: "An agreement between two or more persons which creates an obligation to do or not to do a particular thing." (Black, p. 322) Generally, the five basic elements of a contract are: (1) mutual assent (2) by legally competent parties for (3) consideration (4) to subject matter that is legal and (5) in a form of agreement which is legal.

Mutual assent implies that two parties entering into a contract agree to its provisions. A Catholic school agrees to provide an education to a student and the parents accept the education, or a Catholic school offers a teacher a contract which the teacher accepts. *Consideration* is what each party agrees to do for the other party in exchange for something from that party. The Catholic school agrees to provide educational services to a student in return for payment of tuition and adherence to school rules. The school agrees to pay the teacher a salary in return for teaching services.

Legally competent parties are persons who are lawfully qualified to enter into an agreement. School administrators are legally qualified to enter into contracts to educate students and to employ teachers. Parents are legally competent to agree to pay tuition and meet other obligations. Persons under the age of eighteen are not legally competent to enter into educational contracts, so parents must be the contracting parties. A properly qualified teacher is a legally competent party; a person who does not possess the certification or other qualifications needed to teach would not be legally competent to enter into a teaching contract.

Legal subject matter assumes that the provisions of the contract are legal. An agreement that a teacher would not date or marry a person of another race as a condition of employment would not be legal as such a condition would most likely be a violation of anti-discrimination laws.

Legal form may vary from state to state. If any one of the five elements of a contract is missing, the contract may be held to be null and void.

Cases involving student and teacher discipline, particularly dismissal, in Catholic schools often allege breach of contract. Breach of contract can be committed by either party to the contract. It is generally conceded, however, that it is futile for a school administrator to bring breach of contract charges against a teacher who wants to terminate a contract. Judges will not compel persons to teach against their will. Historically, courts have not compelled performance of a contract for personal services, which one party no longer wishes to perform, since a contractual arrangement is seen as a private arrangement. Courts will not force persons to associate with each other. The remedy for breach of contract is damages, not specific performance.

While teachers can usually break their contracts without severe consequences, schools and administrators who terminate a teacher's employment during a contract term without just cause or who terminate a student's enrollment without just cause can ordinarily expect to pay damages if a lawsuit is filed.

The relationship of schools to students has been compared to that of fiduciaries, persons who are supposed to take at least as much care of that which is entrusted to them as they would take of their own property. This theory, first postulated in 1957, seems to be echoed in more recent cases holding school officials to strict standards of care. Professor Warren Seavey in an article in the *Harvard Law Review* in 1957 argued that public institutions have clear responsibilities to students. He wrote:

> It is shocking that the officials of a state educational institution, which can function properly only if our freedoms are preserved, should not understand the elementary principles of fair play. It is equally shocking to find that a court supports them in denying to a student the protection given to a pickpocket. (p. 1407)

All administrators, whether public or private, should seek to treat students fairly and in the manner in which they would wish to be treated themselves. A fiduciary is charged with showing that whatever is done is done honestly. This approach would shift the burden of proof from the student to the institution. One can see elements of the common law and fundamental fairness arguments here. A reasonable individual would expect that a person or institution charged with the care of others would exercise that care or be able to show just cause why such care was not given.

Duties of Administrators

Not too long ago the administration of a school was invested in the principal alone. Assistant principals were found, if at all, in the high school. Today assistant principals are a necessary and welcome addition to the ranks of school administrators. Every school needs a "second in command" who can advise the principal, carry out delegated duties and act with authority in the principal's absence. Principals should appoint as assistants only those persons whom they trust. Team administration is practically a necessity in these times when schools are meeting much more than simple education needs. It is important that handbooks and other documents clearly delineate the responsibilities and authority of assistant principals and principals.

Administrators generally have numerous duties and responsibilities, many of which are not clearly defined in any document. The safest course might be for principals to assume that they are responsible for everything that happens in their schools. The principal may delegate decision-making powers to others, such as assistant principals, but the responsibility cannot be delegated. If a lawsuit were filed against a school and/or a teacher, it is virtually certain that the principal would be sued as well. In parish-sponsored schools, pastors will be sued; bishops are sued when diocesan-owned schools are sued.

The duties of principals can be summarized under two headings: (1) policy formation and communication of rules and policies; and (2) supervision of personnel. Almost every responsibility of a principal can be placed under one of these two categories.

Even though pastors, school boards and superintendents may have the final responsibility for ultimately approving policy, the principal should play a crucial role in developing it. It is hard to imagine a school board, for example, writing and approving policy without seeking the principal's input. The principal is the educational expert who is charged with communication and implementation of policy. It makes little sense for the principal to have no role in its development. Current data suggest that the national trend at the elementary school is towards advisory boards and councils, rather than policy-making boards. The advisory board can be extremely helpful in the development and recommendation of policy.

One of the principal's most serious responsibilities is the supervision of teachers. It is crucial that administrators, teachers and board members understand that supervision and evaluation of teachers are the principal's and, if the principal chooses, the assistant principal's responsibility. The principal is supposed to ensure that students have the best possible educational experience. In reality, supervision is quality control for the school.

Supervision is not only determining that persons are performing their assigned tasks in a satisfactory manner; it is also job protection for the teacher. If a principal does not supervise a teacher and allegations are later made about the competency of the teacher, the principal will have no evidence against which to judge the allegation. If a teacher is faced with a malpractice suit charging failure to teach, the principal is the person best equipped to assist the teacher in meeting these charges. Principals have many duties, but none is more important than supervision. A principal who fails to supervise is professionally negligent and may be found liable for injuries occurring due to a teacher's actions that proper supervision might have identified and remediated.

Duties of Teachers

The duties of teachers can also be classified under two headings: (1) implementing school rules and policies and (2) supervising the safety and learning of students. Teachers should understand that their job is to implement rules, even if they do not personally agree with them. Lack of agreement is not a reason to fail to enforce a rule. If a teacher cannot support a given rule or policy, that teacher can use whatever channels exist to modify the rule, but until a change is made, the teacher is obligated to follow the directive. If a person cannot, in conscience, support the action required and change is not possible, that individual's only real choice may be to resign.

Supervision of student safety and learning has both mental and physical implications. It is not enough for a teacher to be bodily present; the teacher must concentrate on the students. Some student accidents and injuries could be avoided if teachers paid closer attention to the students. Recent cases involving student injuries have alleged, not that the teacher was absent, but rather that the teacher was present but not paying attention.

Conclusion

Civil law is multi-faceted and school administrators may be tempted to leave legal matters to lawyers. But lawyers can only give guidance. It is the administrator who makes the day-to-day decisions that determine liability. Every administrator needs at least a basic working knowledge of civil law as it applies to Catholic schools. That working knowledge will be invaluable in the development of school handbooks.

CHAPTER TWO—
NEGLIGENCE

If a school administrator is sued, there is a high degree of probability that the suit will be one alleging negligence. Even though negligence is the "fault" against which administrators must guard most constantly, it is also one of the most difficult types of case about which to predict an accurate judicial outcome. What may be considered negligence in one court may not be so considered in another. It is much better, obviously, to avoid being accused of negligence in the first place than to take one's chances on the outcome of a lawsuit. Negligence can be either acts of commission or "sins" of omission. The negligent individual either did something he should not have done or failed to do something she should have done.

There are four elements which must be present before legal negligence can exist. These elements, which have been defined by many legal writers, are: duty, violation of duty, proximate cause and injury. If any one of the four elements is missing, no legal negligence can be found. Since negligence is the unintentional act which results in an injury, a person charged with negligence is generally not going to face criminal charges or spend time in prison.

An examination of each of the four elements necessary to constitute a finding of negligence is helpful. First, the person charged with negligence must have had a duty in the situation. Students have a right to safety, and teachers and administrators have a responsibility to protect the safety of all entrusted to their care. Teachers are expected to provide reasonable supervision of students. Administrators should develop rules and regulations which guide teachers in providing for student safety. Teachers will generally not be held responsible for injuries occurring at a place where, or at a time when, they had no responsibility. A student injured on the way to school, for example, normally will not be able to demonstrate that a teacher or administrator had a duty to protect that individual.

However, administrators should be aware of the fact that courts may hold them responsible for student behavior and its consequences occurring on school property before or after school. The presence of students on school grounds before school opens or after the school day ends is extremely problematic for administrators. In an early, but very important case, *Titus v. Lindberg* 228 A. 2d 65 (New Jersey, 1967), the administrator was found liable for student injury occurring on school grounds before school because: he knew that students arrived on the grounds before the doors were opened; he was present on the campus when they were; he had established no rules for student conduct outside the building and he had not provided for supervision of the students. The court found that the principal had a reasonable duty to provide such supervision when he knew that students were on the property at unauthorized times as a regular practice.

The *Titus* case illustrates the dilemma in which school administrators may find themselves. If a parent drops a student off at the school at 6:30 a.m. and the school opens at 7:00 a.m., is the administrator responsible for the student? How does the administrator provide for supervision? Should supervision be provided? There are no easy answers to the problems of supervision of students before school, after school, and while waiting for activities to begin. But the administrator must develop some policy and/or procedures to deal with the reality that students will be present at unauthorized times.

It is important to keep in mind that the court will look at the reasonableness of the administrator's behavior. Is it reasonable to expect that an administrator will provide for the supervision of students on school grounds no matter how early they arrive and/or how late they stay? Probably no court would expect an administrator to be present at 6:00 a.m.; however, the court will expect some policy or statement as to when students may arrive on campus, what rules they are to follow, and what kind of supervision will be provided.

Common sense also has to prevail. If the administrator arrives at school thirty minutes before the doors open and a child is standing outside in sub-zero weather, the reasonable person would bring the child indoors. A court might well find in a situation in which a child is standing outside in freezing weather that the administrator had a duty to protect the child from harm.

The second element involved in negligence is *violation of duty*. Negligence cannot exist if the administrator or teacher has not violated a duty. Courts expect that accidents and spontaneous actions can occur. If a teacher is properly supervising a playground at recess, and one child picks up a rock and throws it and so injures another child, the teacher cannot be held liable. However, if a teacher who is responsible for the supervision of the playground were to allow rock throwing to continue without attempting to stop it and a student were injured, the teacher would probably be held liable. Similarly, a teacher who leaves a classroom unattended in order to take a coffee break will generally be held to have violated a duty. But if it can be demonstrated that teachers have, as a general practice, taken coffee breaks and left classes unattended, and, because of the inattention or inaction of the principal, nothing was done about the situation, the principal may be held equally, if not more, liable than the teacher.

The third requirement of negligence is that the violation of duty must be the proximate cause of the injury. In other words, would the injury have occurred if proper supervision had been present? The jury has to decide whether proper supervision could have prevented the injury and, in so deciding, has to look at the facts of each individual case.

The tragic case of *Levandoski v. Jackson City School District* 328 So. 2d 339 (Minnesota, 1976) illustrates. In this case, a teacher failed to report that a thirteen-year-old girl was missing from class. The child was later found murdered some distance from the school. The child's mother alleged that, if the child's absence had been reported, the murder would not have happened. However, the court found that no evidence existed to show that if the teacher and principal had properly and promptly reported the child's absence, the murder could have been prevented. One should not conclude that carelessness in reporting absences is not a serious matter; had the child been found on the school premises, there is a high likelihood that the teacher would have been found negligent. The *Levandoski* court simply found that the teacher's violation of duty was the not the proximate cause of the student's death.

The well-known case of *Smith v. Archbishop of St. Louis*, 632 S.W. 2d 516 (Missouri Court of Appeals, 1982), involving a Catholic school, illustrates the concept of proximate cause. A second grade teacher kept a lighted candle on her desk every morning during May in honor of the Mother of God. She gave no special instructions to the students regarding the dangers of a lighted candle. One day, a student who was wearing a crepe paper costume, got too close to the candle and her costume caught fire. The teacher had difficulty putting out the flames, and the child sustained facial and upper body burns such that during the five years the litigation was in process, she underwent several operations and numerous painful treatments. The child sustained psychological as well as physical damage and experts testified that she would likely experience a lifetime of psychological problems. The appellate court upheld an award for damages and a finding of negligent supervision against the archdiocese. This case demonstrates the liability that can accrue to a Catholic school and to a diocese because of the negligence of a teacher or an administrator.

The *Smith* case also illustrates the concept of *foreseeability*. The plaintiff did not have to prove that the defendant could foresee that a particular injury (plaintiff's costume catching fire) had to occur; the plaintiff had to establish that a reasonable person would have foreseen that injuries could result from having an unattended lighted candle in a second grade classroom when no safety instructions had been given to the students.

In determining whether a teacher's behavior was reasonable, a court might ask the following questions: (1) Had the teacher given the student clear instructions as to how to behave in his or her absence? (2) Was the teacher absent a reasonable length of time? Five minutes seem reasonable; a thirty-minute absence during which a teacher took a coffee break, made a phone call, or copied papers would probably not be considered reasonable.

In determining whether the principal would be liable for accidents occurring during a teacher's absence, a court might pose these questions: (1) Has the principal developed a clear policy for teachers who need to leave classrooms? (2) Has the principal implemented the policy? (3) Has he or she supervised teachers to make sure that they are following the policy? From the above discussion, it should be apparent that negligence is a complex concept. It is often difficult to predict what a court will consider proximate cause in any particular allegation of negligence.

The fourth element necessary for a finding of negligence is injury. No matter how irresponsible the behavior of a teacher or administrator, there is no legal negligence if there is no injury. If a teacher leaves twenty first-graders unsupervised near a lake and no one is injured, there can be no finding of negligence. Any reasonable person, though, can see that no one in authority should take risks that may result in injury.

Most negligence cases occur in the classroom because that is where students and teachers spend most of their time. However, there are other areas that are potentially more dangerous than the classroom and, hence, a greater standard of teacher and administrator care will be expected.

Lab and physical education classes, for example, contain greater potential for injury, and case law indicates that courts expect teachers to exercise greater caution there than they would in ordinary classrooms. Teachers and administrators are also expected to maintain equipment in working order and to keep areas free of unnecessary hazards. Teachers should also give students safety instructions regarding the use of potentially dangerous equipment.

Athletic programs pose special problems. Even if every possible precaution were taken, the possibility for student injury during athletics is very high. Administrators, who sometimes may be tempted to let athletic directors and coaches worry about athletic programs, have very real duties to ensure that: competent, properly trained personnel serve as coaches for teams; that clear procedures are followed when accidents occur; that equipment and playing areas are as hazard-free as possible.

The younger the child, the greater the educator's responsibility. It might be acceptable to leave a group of high school seniors alone for ten minutes in a math class when it would not be acceptable to leave a group of first graders alone. It is reasonable to expect that fifteen-year-olds of average intelligence could observe traffic signals when they are crossing a street. It would not be reasonable to expect mentally disabled fifteen-year-olds to be responsible for crossing the street.

In developing and implementing policies for supervision, the educator must keep in mind the reasonableness standard and ask, "Is this what one would expect a reasonable person in a similar situation to do?" No one expects a principal or a teacher to think of every possible situation that might occur. A court would not necessarily consider it unreasonable if a school did not have a rule prohibiting throwing chairs; the court would expect, though, that there would be some sort of rule encompassing the possibility of such an activity. No one can foresee everything that might happen, but reasonable persons can assume that certain situations are potentially dangerous. The teacher in the *Smith* case should have foreseen that an open flame might cause injury to second-graders.

The best defense for an administrator in a negligence suit is the development of reasonable policies and rules for the safety of those entrusted to his or her care. The reasonable administrator is one who supervises teachers and others in their implementation of rules.

The prudent administrator must take an offensive approach with regard to the elimination of hazards. All activities should be carefully monitored. All staff, paid and volunteer, should receive thorough and ongoing orientation and instruction. The administrator who practices prevention by constantly striving to eliminate foreseeable risks will avoid both injuries and costly litigation.

CHAPTER THREE—
PRINCIPLES OF HANDBOOK PREPARATION

Know the Law

Although Catholic school administrators are usually not lawyers, they are the persons responsible for the "lawful" operation of the school and the ones who can be held legally liable for activities or omissions. It is true that most administrators will never face personal liability for actions or omissions; however, principals will want to avoid both personal liability and liability as an agent of the school. An informed administrator can help ensure that policies and procedures comply with existing law and will know enough to seek competent legal advice when it is needed.

Most college and university principalship preparation programs require that students take at least one course in school law. Unfortunately, the vast majority of school law courses are geared to public schools. As Chapter One indicated, the laws affecting public schools and those affecting Catholic schools can be very different. Administrators who have not had a course in non-public school law should read texts on the topic, such as this one and have a set of resources, including books and articles available.

Most attorneys do not have any special training or experience in private school law and may not be aware, for example, that while in Catholic schools, persons do not have Constitutional protections. A tax attorney who sits on a school board may not be the best choice for a school law advisor. Principals should always be willing to discuss situations with the diocesan office personnel who can direct them to competent legal advisors, such as the diocesan attorney.

There is an old saying that sometimes the best knowledge is knowing what you don't know. School law is one example of that maxim. What you don't know *can* hurt you, especially where the law is concerned. The wise principal will read current articles on Catholic school legal issues, participate in workshops and seek advice when necessary.

Having a competent attorney review contractual documents, including handbooks, for legal soundness is an excellent practice. Principals should budget adequate funds for access to good legal services.

Be Able to Apply the Law

All the knowledge in the world won't help school administrators if they can't apply the law. Applying the law is not unlike driving a car. It's a skill. Administrators have to practice. After reading an article on field trips, an administrator should ask, "How does this apply to my situation? Are my school's policies and procedures in line with the principles expressed in the article? Are we doing some things here that could be legally problematic?"

Inbaskets are a popular learning tool. Participants bring or are given some real life problem situations and asked to determine how they would handle them. Role-playing provides much the same opportunity. Having a mentor or a peer partner is also a help. When faced with a potential legal problem, the administrator who can "talk the situation through" with another administrator will generally be more confident and able to meet challenges.

Know the Situation

The administrator is the expert on his or her school. This author often asks persons who call for advice, "What do you want to do?" before rendering an opinion. Some people are startled and say, "But I called you to find out what to do." The administrator knows his or her school and is well acquainted with its particularities.

The question, which needs to be answered, is generally *not*, "What can I legally do?" but rather, "Given what I can legally do, what should I do?" Just because a certain course of action is legally permissible doesn't mean it is the right thing to do. For example, it may be perfectly legal to tell a twenty-five year teacher that her contract is not being renewed without giving any reason, but it may not be the right thing to do. Ethical and moral questions must be addressed as well as legal ones.

Protect the School Contractually

Contract law is the basic source of the law in Catholic schools. Handbooks can be, and generally are, considered contracts. Thus, principals must ensure that actions taken comply with existing policies and procedures. If students facing suspension are entitled to a hearing, the principal should not suspend them without having a hearing, no matter how heinous the offense or how much at wit's-end the principal is. Courts scrutinize contractual documents in cases involving private schools. The legal principle is generally that the document is construed in favor of the non-writing party. Therefore, principals must ensure that policies are clear and leave little room for arguments over interpretation. Further, principals must act in ways that are consistent with contractual documents as well as with commonly accepted standards of good faith and fair dealing as discussed in the previous chapter.

Do Not Make Promises That Cannot Be Kept

In today's troubled times, parents want assurances that their children are safe. While making every effort to keep children safe, principals must be careful not to promise too much. Principals should not guarantee the safety of children because principals cannot control every factor that influences safety.

Safety is a prominent issue. There are others. The principle is, do not promise what cannot be delivered.

Always have an "escape" clause

No matter how careful the handbook writer and/or principal, situations will arise that were not anticipated or which call for different responses than the handbook delineates. There should always be a right to suspend and a right to amend clause such as the following: "The principal is the final recourse and reserves the right to amend this handbook. Parents will be given prompt notification."

Keeping Up With Handbook Development and Revision

The task of handbook development and revision can appear daunting. But, like many other tasks, it can be accomplished incrementally. Administrators may want to consider using an index card or computer entry approach. Every time the administrator thinks of something to add or revise in the handbook, the idea is entered onto an index card or into a computer file. Staff can be invited to submit ideas for addition, deletion and revision as well. If such an approach is utilized, the administrator has a resource bank from which to draw when it is time to write or revise the handbook.

CHAPTER FOUR—
FACULTY HANDBOOKS

The faculty handbook should be a kind of bible for faculty and administrators. Both should be thoroughly familiar with its contents. Unfortunately, too many faculty members do not know the contents of the handbook and, worse, sometimes cannot even locate it. A good faculty handbook is an investment of time and talent in the smooth operation of the school. The administrator who refers to the handbook and who holds faculty accountable for the policies and procedures contained therein will help ensure the realization of the school's mission.

There are several approaches to organizing the contents of a handbook. Some administrators prefer an alphabetical approach; such an approach can certainly make finding items in a handbook easier. However, an administrator could decide that a topical arrangement is more suitable to a given school's needs.

A Faculty Handbook Checklist, utilizing a topical format, follows. The administrator may wish to copy this checklist and use it to make notes as this chapter is read and as handbook development or revision is planned. The checklist can be shared with faculty and board members as their input is gathered.

FACULTY HANDBOOK CHECKLIST

What should a school have?   *What does my school need?*

Mission Statement
Administration
Instructional Duties
Non-Instructional Duties
Supervision and Evaluation
Personnel Policies
Personal Behavior
Boundary Issues
Confidentiality
Custody Issues
Child Abuse
Harassment
Violence
Sample Forms

SCHOOL MISSION STATEMENT

The school mission statement should be the basis for all policies and procedures. Ideally, the life of the school should be seen as flowing from the mission statement. Basically, the Catholic school mission statement answers the questions, "Why does this school exist?" and "What do we as Catholic educators say that we are doing in this school?"

Parents, teachers and courts expect that the rules and regulations of a school will be consistent with the stated mission of the school. Therefore, the administrator should review policies and proposed policy changes in light of the mission statement.

Most schools have mission statements, and all should have them. The mission statement should be reviewed at least once a year so that the school's performance can be evaluated in light of the mission statement. Significant problem areas should be settled, so that each year all members of the school community can "own" the mission statement and those policies and procedures which emanate from it.

What about schools that do not have mission statements? The administrator should begin the process of developing one with the school community. The mission statement provides a gauge for determining policies and procedures and for measuring success in attaining them. It would be difficult to justify a policy that is clearly at odds with the mission of the school; furthermore, the mission statement should guide the development of all policies and procedures.

ADMINISTRATION

Every principal should have an assistant principal, even if the assistant principal also has full-time teaching duties. The assistant's duties should be delineated and the scope of the assistant's authority should be identified. The assistant should be fully empowered to act in the principal's absence. Assistants may share in supervisory and evaluation duties, may be responsible for schedule development, and may have other duties.

INSTRUCTIONAL DUTIES

It might seem that instructional duties should occupy the bulk of the handbook. Certainly, those duties are the ones that are uppermost in the minds of administrators writing or revising handbooks. There are at least three main areas of instructional duties.

Instruction of Students

Teachers should be clearly told what they are expected to do with regard to instruction of students. It is not necessary to dictate *how* teachers are to do everything, but it is necessary to delineate some broad guidelines as to *what* they are to accomplish. If state law mandates competency or achievement testing, some discussion of appropriate instructional strategies may be offered. Persons to be consulted for help and direction, such as department heads and assistant principals, should be identified

Supervision of Students

A second area might be concerned with supervision of students within the learning situation. Supervision outside the regular classroom learning setting would be discussed under non-instructional duties. Teacher responsibility for students in the classroom should be thoroughly discussed. The fact that supervision is mental, i.e., the person has to be paying attention to the students, as well as physical, i.e., the teacher is physically present, should be stressed. In the 1980s, cases involving student injuries often alleged that teachers were absent when injuries occurred; in the 1990s many cases alleged not that the teacher was absent, but rather that the teacher was present, but not paying attention to the students.

Procedures for leaving students unattended should be discussed. There are situations, such as emergencies, that could require a teacher to leave a classroom unattended. Courts recognize this fact; however, judges and juries do expect that students will not be left without directions as to behavioral expectations. One standard courts use is: the younger the child chronologically or mentally, the greater the standard of care. The second standard is the reasonable teacher standard. Did the teacher act the way a reasonable teacher would be expected to act? The reasonable teacher standard is applied equally to all teachers, the twenty-five year veteran as well as the first year novice. Juries determine whether an individual's actions are those of a reasonable teacher. If a teacher must leave the students, what procedures should be followed? How should the teacher ensure that students know what to do in the absence of the teacher?

Record-Keeping/Grading

A third area involving instructional duties is that of record-keeping and grading. The handbooks should state what factors are to be considered in the determination of grades. Letter grades and numerical equivalents should be defined.

Teachers should know what their responsibilities are with regard to record keeping. How long should attendance records be kept? States have different requirements, but, at the minimum, attendance records should be kept for at least five years after the student graduates or leaves the school. There have been cases in which the police and courts have asked for verification of a student's attendance on a particular day, even several years after an alleged incident occurred. If it is possible to keep the attendance records indefinitely, on computer disks, for example, the administrator should require that they be kept.

Unless the school retains custody of grade books, teachers should keep their grade books in the event of a lawsuit requiring verification of a grade. Conflicts regarding grades can be avoided if there is a policy in place stating that any request for consideration of a grade change must be made within a given number of days after the receipt of the report card.

Teachers should keep their plan books on file in the event that educational malpractice suits are filed against them. The plan book will indicate that the teacher did follow the curriculum and did teach whatever concepts were required.

Professionalism/Loyalty

Teachers are professionals, and all professionals need to be periodically reminded of the expectations of the profession and of their duties to their employer. While people routinely expect professionalism from doctors and lawyers, teachers may believe that the public does not regard them as true professionals. What teachers and other employees do reflects on the school that employs them and care must be taken to do nothing that would reflect unfavorably on the school.

NON-INSTRUCTIONAL DUTIES

Unfortunately, non-instructional duties claim a significant amount of teacher time. An administrator might want to utilize the index card method and begin recording everything a teacher is expected to do that is not, strictly speaking, an instructional duty. Even if the school has a handbook, this exercise might be helpful in ensuring completeness of enumerated duties.

Supervision

Some non-instructional duties come immediately to mind. In the elementary school, teachers are generally assigned to supervise the playground and cafeteria. What exactly are playground supervisors supposed to do? For example, they may be expected to be present on the playground from one bell to the next. Procedures for accidents and reporting fights or other disturbances should be included.

Junior and senior high school teachers might be assigned cafeteria or student hall presiding. The same types of questions should be answered for these teachers. The handbook should clearly state that teachers are not to leave students unattended except for an emergency situation and then only if students know what to do in the teacher's absence.

Student Discipline

Teachers are expected to enforce student discipline. The faculty handbook should contain the student disciplinary code in its entirety, even if it is printed in a separate handbook for parents and/or students, so that teachers have all policies and procedures readily accessible in one place. The disciplinary actions that are reserved to the principal or assistant principal should be outlined.

Field Trip Policies and Procedures

Field trips can be problematic, but virtually all teachers would agree that field trips can be very worthwhile learning experiences. All steps necessary for taking a field trip should be discussed in detail.

Courts are unanimous in ruling that field trips must have an educational purpose. This purpose should be noted on the field trip permission form. The school form should be included and teachers should be instructed that no other form is permitted. The form should include (1) parent request for child's participation; (2) parent permission for participation; (3) parent release of the school from liability for injury in consideration for the child's participation in the field trip; and (4) a statement of the educational purpose of the trip. Procedures to check for forgery of parental signatures should be identified.

Extra-Curricular Activities

Teachers are often expected to sponsor some sort of extra-curricular activity. These activities can range from directing candy drives and Christmas plays to coaching sports. The faculty handbook should state the school's expectations regarding teacher supervision of extra-curricular activities. Can each teacher be required to moderate one or more activities without additional pay? Will the more time-consuming activities carry compensation and, if so, what is the scale of that compensation?

The responsibilities of extra-curricular moderators should be described. Activities such as dances might benefit from a checklist-type approach so that teachers can easily see if they have met their responsibilities.

Attendance at Meetings and other School Events

A final area of non-instructional duties consists of meetings. What meetings are teachers expected to attend? Parent/teacher conferences? PTA meetings? School plays? dances? athletic events? It might be helpful to publish a yearly list of meetings that teachers are responsible for attending. Administrators should reserve the right to require attendance at other meetings in the course of the year. Perhaps a statement that, as far as possible, a certain number of days' notice will be given, would be helpful.

SUPERVISION AND EVALUATION OF TEACHERS

Supervision and evaluation of teachers are matters of personnel policy. Since these activities are most important for both faculty and administrators, a separate section is devoted to them.

Frequency and Format

Administrators have a responsibility to supervise and evaluate teachers. Teachers have the right to know how often they can expect to be supervised and what format the report of the supervisory visit will take. Supervision can be problematic for both the principal and the teacher. A principal who never taught any grade below sixth, for example, may feel inadequate in a primary teacher's classroom; a high school principal who taught English may feel less than competent in a physics classroom. However, administrators and all effective educators should be able to recognize good teaching. If a principal is clearly "out of" his or her league in a certain content area, the assistance of someone with subject area competency can be sought.

If supervision is an ongoing, formative process, both principal and teacher can grow together and help each other to improve the learning environment of the school. If supervision is viewed as punitive, as something that is only engaged in if the principal is "out to get" the teacher, it will hardly be successful.

Evaluation is *summative*: an administrator sums up all the available data and makes a decision regarding contract renewal. Evaluation of teaching performance, then, should be based on more than supervisory data. A principal will seek to answer such questions as: does this teacher support the rules of the school? Does he or she look after the safety of the children as well as, "Is he or she a good subject matter teacher?" Evaluation, then, is a broader concept than supervision, but both should be present in a good school. The demands placed upon administrators make it easy to defer supervision, but supervision should be one of the primary tasks of the principal.

All school administrators must understand that teachers and administrators are in school for the students; the students are not there for the adults' employment. Surely, there is no more sacred responsibility than ensuring that students are being taught by capable, competent, caring professionals and that all teachers are encouraged and given the means to become the best professionals they can be. Ultimately, it is the principal who is responsible for supervision and evaluation of teachers even if someone else, such as the pastor, signs the contract. Supervision and evaluation enable a principal to make sound decisions about contract renewal. It is not just for a principal to decline to renew a teacher s contract if the principal has never observed the teacher.

Written observations that have been shared with teachers provide some of the best data for making employment decisions. A principal can use the data to plan and set goals with teachers. The handbook should state the school policy on supervision of teachers. Who is responsible for supervising teachers? Is it the principal's sole responsibility, or are other persons, such as assistant principals, department heads or others involved? How often will the teacher be supervised? What format will be used?

Scheduled v. Unscheduled Visits

Will the supervisor's visits be scheduled or unscheduled? If the visits are normally scheduled for twice a year, does the principal reserve the right to observe classes at unscheduled times? The teacher also has a right to know how evaluation will occur. How will the supervisory visit data be incorporated into the end-of-the-year evaluation? Who will see this evaluation? Will the evaluation become part of the teacher's permanent file? Does the teacher have an opportunity to respond in writing to the evaluation? Will the teacher's response become part of the evaluation record? Considering these questions and developing policies to answer them will help an administrator operate on solid legal ground.

Although most educators would agree that supervision is a *formative* experience and evaluation is a *summative* one, the distinction becomes blurred in many Catholic schools where the principal and/or assistant principal serves as both supervisor and evaluator. These dual responsibilities can pose very real problems. Teachers may be reluctant to discuss problems with principals if they suspect that the information could be used against them in evaluations. Catholic school administrators who are both supervisors and evaluators should be especially sensitive to the issues posed by this dual role.

PERSONNEL POLICIES

The personnel policies of the school should be found in the faculty handbook. The reasons for which teachers may be absent from school represent a major personnel policy issue.

Sick Days, Personal Days, Jury and Military Duty

What policy does the school have with regard to sick days and personal days? Can unused sick leave accumulate? If it can, is there an upward limit of accumulation? A good rule of thumb might be ten days of sick leave and one or two personal days. Allowing persons to accumulate sick leave can help guard against some teachers taking sick leave simply because if they don't take it, they lose it.

A personal day is an absence for which a person does not have to provide a specific reason. Policy can place certain parameters around personal days, such as, they cannot be taken the day before or after major holidays. If persons are required to state the reasons for requesting personal days, those days should be named something other than personal. Some schools allow for emergency days. Other necessary absences could result from jury duty or military duty, such as the reserves of the armed forces. Persons have a legal right to perform jury duty and principals have no right to require a teacher to request a deferment to a time when school is not in session. A principal can request a teacher to seek a deferment of jury duty but may not penalize a teacher who does not seek a deferment.

Military Duty

Teachers who serve in the reserves of the Armed Forces must report for duty when called. Although this statement may seem obvious, there are administrators who mistakenly attempt to thwart or defer a teacher's military duty. Despite the inconvenience to the school, the teacher does have to serve and may not be penalized in any way for serving. Members of the Armed Forces are legally entitled to return to the same or substantially similar jobs when they complete military service.

Parental Leave

The issue of parental leave must be addressed. Courts have held that women may continue working throughout their pregnancies, so long as they are able to perform their duties. Pregnancy is not a disability. Women are able to use all vacation and sick time. They are also able to use the Family and Medical Leave Act which allows up to ninety days leave, which can be unpaid after the exhaustion of vacation and sick time. Fathers are able to use accrued sick and vacation time, as well as to access the Family and Medical Leave Act. There have been instances in which principals have denied or attempted to deny adoptive mothers parental leave on the mistaken theory that the purpose of maternity leave is to recover from delivery. Federal and most state laws require that whatever leave is available for persons who give birth be made available to those who adopt since one of the main purposes of parental leave is to bond with one's child.

Bereavement Leave

Bereavement leave is another potential source for misunderstanding and comparison making. It is wise, therefore, to state how many days off are allowed and for what degree of kinship. It is generally accepted that a person is allowed time off for the death of a spouse's relative within the same degree of kinship, such as parent, sibling, grandparents, as would be allowed for one's own relatives. If exceptions can be made, the person responsible for making the exception should be named. In all policies regarding leave, the principal might wish to add a line stating that the limits of the leave can be extended at administrative discretion. Such a statement allows for situations in which the rules simply do not seem to apply. Administrators must be careful to make exceptions only when circumstances warrant them and to avoid the appearance of favoritism. From an ethical and compassionate viewpoint, it seems better to err on the side of compassion than on strict adherence to policy.

Grievance Procedures

No matter how hard administrators try to be fair in their

dealings with faculty, honest disagreements can and do arise. Canon law encourages persons to practice *subsidiarity*, the solving of problems at the lowest possible level. Sometimes agreement cannot be reached between principal and teacher. In extreme cases, grievances may be filed. If the school or the diocese or the religious congregation does not have a grievance procedure, the principal, pastor, or other person with appropriate authority should initiate a plan to develop one. What constitutes matter for a grievance should be clearly defined. All disagreements between teachers and administrators are not grievances.

The grievance procedure should contain, at minimum, the following sections: (1) definition of terms, (2) purpose of the procedure, (3) steps in the procedure and (4) identification of the parties and levels of grievance, including which party has the final word.

Tenure/Job Protection

Job protection is important to teachers. Since the 1979 United States Supreme Court case, *National Labor Relations Board v. Catholic Bishop of Chicago,* 440 U.S. 490, Catholic schools are not required to allow unionization of employees. Unions in existence prior to this ruling remain in place. Although Catholic schools generally do not have formal tenure systems and, indeed, many contracts are year-to-year, in the past a situation called *de facto* tenure was sometimes found. In fact, many teachers in Catholic schools do have an expectation of continuing employment.

If a Catholic school dismissed a teacher who had been working in the school for ten years, the court would examine the policies, procedures and past practices of the school system. If teachers are usually retained in the system after three years and rarely, if ever, face non-renewal of contract, *de facto* tenure may exist. However, the concept of *de facto* tenure appears to be dying as a legal argument to protect teacher employment.

Termination and/or Non-Renewal of Contract

Most cases involving teachers in both the public and private sectors are concerned with teacher dismissals and/or the non-renewal of contracts. Obviously, a decision to dismiss or not renew the contract of a teacher is one that an administrator should not make lightly, and it is one that should be made only after other attempts at discipline of the faculty member have failed. Although the Constitutional protections afforded public school teachers are not available to Catholic school teachers, contract law protects both sets of teachers. Administrators in both schools must honor the provisions of the contract made with the teacher or be able to give legitimate reasons for breaking the contract.

Courts will scrutinize both public and private school contracts to ensure that the provisions of the contract have been followed. While a Catholic school contract may be far less involved than a public school contract, it is nonetheless a contract. Courts can also construe handbooks and policy statements as part of the contract existing between teacher and employer and can hold school officials to the provisions of both documents.

Public school teachers may be discharged for reasons generally found in state law. Some of these reasons are incapacity, incompetence, insubordination, unprofessional conduct, immorality and others. A quick survey of the laws of any state will reveal the problems inherent in defining causes for dismissal. What is incompetence? Who decides what it is? When is it serious enough to warrant dismissal of the teacher? The following discussion of reasons often found given for public school dismissals may be helpful to Catholic school administrators.

Incapacity is a term that can encompass any of several conditions, including physical or mental incapacity which is permanent and incurable, although federal laws prohibiting discrimination against persons with disabilities must be observed.

Incompetence can be: lack of knowledge about the subject matter one is contracted to teach or lack of ability to impart that knowledge; inability to adapt to new teaching methods; physical, sexual, or verbal mistreatment of students; disregard of school rules; failure to perform reasonable duties; refusal to support the school administration; negligent conduct; and personal misconduct.

Insubordination is generally the willful refusal to abide by the rules or the directives of superiors. It can be distinguished from incompetence in that an incompetent person may be involved in the same behavior as an insubordinate person, but the incompetent person is not assumed to be willfully violating duties and rules.

Unprofessional conduct can also encompass a wide range of behaviors. Unprofessional conduct may be the same behavior as personal misconduct. However, while all personal misconduct is unprofessional conduct, not all unprofessional conduct is personal misconduct. For example, it might be considered unprofessional conduct to discuss school matters with friends, but it would be difficult to put that behavior in the same category as personal misconduct, such as sexual offenses or driving while intoxicated.

Immorality is listed in the statutes of many states as grounds for dismissal. However, different communities have different standards of morality and those standards change with time. Case law indicates that courts differ in their interpretation of what constitutes immorality and what constitutes unfitness to teach. Some courts have held that performing an immoral act may not be justification for terminating employment unless proof is available that the act somehow affects one's ability to teach. More recent case law, however, appears to be divided, particularly in instances involving sexual misconduct. Standards of fitness are changing. Catholic school administrators can, of course, enforce much stricter standards of behavior than public school administrators can. Some states include "catch all" phrases such as, "a teacher may be dismissed for any other just cause." Just as administrators are not expected to think of everything which a student could possibly do in the way of misconduct or violation of school rules, state legislatures are not expected to provide for every occasion that may result in the dismissal of a teacher. Courts often apply the "whole record" test in teacher dismissal cases, except in situations such as criminal conviction or other gross misconduct. If an administrator is seeking to dismiss a teacher for incompetence, the dismissal will probably not be upheld if it is based on a single incident. The court will consider the whole record of the teacher involved before rendering a decision.

Since public school teachers are bound by contract to observe statutes governing them, a teacher who violates any of the prescribed rules can be legitimately dismissed. At the same time, the administrator would have the responsibility of providing reasonable evidence as proof of the validity of claims. Similarly, Catholic and other private school teachers are bound to the terms of their contract or agreement with the institution that employs them. Teacher violations of contract terms in the private institution may legitimately result in dismissal. Catholic school administrators should ensure that the causes for dismissal and the procedures for leading up to dismissal are clearly stated in handbooks. Contracts should include a statement that the faculty member agrees to abide by the regulations in the handbook; as indicated earlier, many courts consider handbooks to be part of the contract.

Policies should not be contradictory. In 1982 five religious sisters in New Hampshire sued the bishop and superintendent of schools (*Reardon et al. v. LeMoyne, et al.* 454 A.2d 428) because their contracts were not renewed. The major problem was the language of the teacher contracts. One clause stated that employment ended each year unless definitively renewed. Another clause contained a statement to the effect that a teacher could expect employment until the summer following his or her seventieth birthday. Clearly, the clauses were contradictory. Problems could have been avoided if the contracts had been checked for possible contradictions. The court ruled that it did have jurisdiction over the civil employment contracts of religious.

The parish school board was ordered to give the sisters a hearing, if the sisters desired one. As one can imagine, this is one of those situations in which everybody loses in some way. The sisters lost their jobs; the parish community felt the effects of the conflict; the diocese, no doubt, was affected as well.

School administrators need to state the school's position on contract renewal in the faculty handbook. Is the contract a year-to-year agreement which grants no expectation of continuing employment? Or is there a kind of *de facto* tenure operative in theory or in practice? It is very important that the handbook and the contract be in harmony. Does a teacher have any recourse in a non-renewal situation? Some schools and dioceses provide for some kind of hearing in an effort to be sure that actions are moral as well as legal. If a hearing is to be granted, the persons constituting the hearing board and the process for conducting a hearing must be clearly defined. The person or group that has the final word must be identified. In many cases, the bishop is the last court of appeal. Regardless of the policy, the best assurance that it will be followed is having it written in the handbook. From a strictly legal standpoint, the best advice is to consider all employment as either "at will" or for the term of the contract, e.g. one year.

PERSONAL BEHAVIOR

Almost every Catholic educational administrator has to face issues of actual or perceived inappropriate staff conduct, and may wonder how to best require appropriate behavior from staff. What a faculty member does, both in and outside the school setting, impacts the quality and integrity of ministry within the setting. The doctrine of separation of church and state protects administrators of religious schools and allows them to set standards of personal behavior that would not be permitted in the public sector. The bottom line is once an individual performs an act that is inconsistent with a teaching position in the Church, that person may no longer be qualified to teach in a Catholic school. The faculty handbook should state that faculty must support the teachings of the Catholic Church and live a life consistent with those teachings.

Illegal Activity

A principal can certainly terminate the employment of an individual who has committed an illegal act. One who is convicted of, or who admits commission of, a crime should be removed from the school. Harder questions arise when a person is simply accused of, or arrested on suspicion of, a crime. The

United States operates under a presumption of innocence. Thus, it may seem that, until guilt is established, the person should be allowed to continue employment. Yet, the reality is often that teacher effectiveness is severely compromised. Principals should strongly consider a policy that allows the administrator to place the accused individual on a leave of absence pending the outcome of an investigation or an adjudication of guilt. Dealing with each situation on an individual basis without some policy is not recommended and leaves an administrator open to charges of arbitrariness and favoritism. It is obviously much easier to deal with an established policy or procedure than it is to try to construct a policy when needed.

BOUNDARY ISSUES

Teacher-Student Relationships

Principals want teachers to care about students and to be interested in their lives. Yet, professional boundaries must be honored. The teacher is not the student's parent or friend. Teachers must understand that they are professionals rendering a service. Just as a counselor or psychiatrist is professionally bound to avoid emotional involvement with a client, a teacher should avoid becoming so emotionally involved with a student that objectivity and fairness are compromised. If a relationship with a student keeps a teacher from responding to other student needs, the principal must insist that the appropriateness of the relationship be examined. In seeking to assess the appropriateness of a relationship, some professionals recommend asking questions such as: Whose needs are being met? Is there a boundary? Where is it? The faculty handbook should contain at least some general guidelines concerning the behaviors expected of teachers. It is not necessary to delineate every possible type of inappropriateness. A statement regarding what it means to be a professional may be sufficient.

CONFIDENTIALITY

Like many other professionals, teachers have long considered confidences to be sacred. If a student confides in a teacher, the student should be able to presume that the confidential information normally will not be shared with anyone. Teachers may believe that they have some type of immunity, which protects them from legal liability, if they refuse to share student information given in confidence, but that belief is mistaken. If a teacher were subpoenaed and asked for information under oath, the judge would require the teacher to answer.

Teachers must make it very clear to students that they will keep their confidences unless health, life or safety is involved; faculty handbooks should require that teachers report such confidences to the appropriate parties. Journal writing, long a staple of the English curriculum, poses real risks of student disclosure of information that the teacher is compelled to reveal. Teachers must set the same rules for confidentiality for journals as for conversations. In the 1995 case of *Brooks v. Logan and Joint District No. 2*, parents of a student who had committed suicide filed claims for wrongful death and negligent infliction of emotion distress against a teacher who had assigned the keeping of journals to her class. The student had written entries indicating that he was depressed and contemplating suicide. The teacher maintained that the student had requested that she not read his entries and so she noted in the journal that she would check only for dates and length. After the student's death, the parents discovered the journal and filed suit. The appellate court ruled that summary judgment was inappropriate and ordered the teacher bound over for trial.

Policy should require that teachers read what students write. If a teacher cannot read the assignment, then the assignment should not be given. In particular, teachers should avoid such techniques as telling students to clip together pages they do not wish the teacher to read or to write at the top of such pages, "Please do not read." Journal writing has a place, but administrators must ensure that teachers set clear parameters for the receipt of student confidences.

CHILD ABUSE

Child abuse is one of the most serious issues confronting educators. The media carry daily reports of adults causing children physical and emotional pain. All fifty states have laws requiring educators to report suspected abuse and/or neglect. The faculty handbook should cite the reporting statutes and should make it very clear that the obligation to report is the teacher's who suspects the abuse, not the administrator's. This author still reads faculty handbooks that instruct the suspecting teacher to notify a school official who will make the report. This procedure is not only dangerous, it is illegal. In addition to statements in the faculty handbook, at least once a year, the principal should review the state child abuse reporting statutes with faculty and staff.

School administrators should provide teachers, other employees and volunteers with some in-service training concerning the indicators of child abuse and neglect and the legal procedures for reporting abuse. There are many excellent written resources available. Local police departments and social service agencies are usually happy to make both materials and speakers available to schools. Principals should decide in advance how visits and requests from police or social workers will be handled and outline those procedures in the faculty handbook. Many states require that school personnel allow officials to examine and question students in the school, often without a school official present. Principals should seek legal counsel in determining the applicable law for a given state.

Abuse by Teachers

The number of lawsuits alleging teacher or other school employee abuse of children is increasing. While administrators can be found responsible for the acts of subordinates, courts appear somewhat unwilling to hold administrators liable for teacher abuse, unless there is clear evidence of administrative misconduct. Many states now mandate that persons who work with children be fingerprinted. Applicants may also be required to sign an authorization of a police check of his or her name for any criminal arrests and/or convictions.

The faculty handbook should indicate the requirements for criminal checks of employees. A student or parent complaint alleging teacher abuse of a child must be taken seriously. Failure to do so can put school officials at grave legal risk. Administrators and school boards should adopt policies governing reporting child abuse/neglect by staff before the need for such policies surfaces. These policies should be clearly outlined in the faculty handbook.

CUSTODY ISSUES

The traditional family of the 1950s is no longer the norm. More than half of all school age children do not live with both biological parents. Custody arrangements pose special challenges for the administrator who is expected to honor court mandated arrangements. Fortunately, some parents do communicate and/or document those arrangements for school officials. Teachers should be informed of custody arrangements affecting their students. The faculty handbook should state the school's expectations for teachers in these matters.

HARASSMENT

Harassment is ongoing demeaning treatment of one who does not consent to the treatment. For as long as there have been students in schools, there has probably been harassment. The student who makes fun of another student's appearance, weight, nationality or disability is guilty of harassment. Faculty must be ever vigilant and guard against all demeaning treatment of students. There is simply no place in a Catholic school for harassment.

Sexual Harassment
Sexual harassment is a familiar topic. School children claim that peers have sexually harassed them. The news stories can seem overwhelming, and the potential for legal liability great. Administrators must ensure, through clear statements in faculty

handbooks, that everyone understands what sexual harassment is. The Equal Employment Opportunities Commission has issued guidelines which define sexual harassment, forbidden by Title VII as: unwelcomed sexual advances, requests for sexual favors, and other verbal or physical conduct of a sexual nature. Another definition is conduct, containing sexual matter or suggestions, which would be offensive to a reasonable person. Most dioceses have sexual abuse/harassment policies and many require that teachers participate in in-service sessions so that they can be fully aware of the regulations and the diocese's expectations of them.

Principals may wish to include the diocesan policy within the text of the faculty handbook as an appendix. Every employee should be required to sign a statement that he or she has been given a copy of the policies relating to sexual harassment and other sexual misconduct, has read the material and agrees to be bound by it. Both faculty and parent/student handbooks should contain at least a general statement that sexual harassment is not condoned in a Christian atmosphere.

VIOLENCE

The relatively recent wave of school shootings has cast fear in the hearts of school administrators. There is no foolproof way to write policies concerning violence so that violence will not occur. The best the administrators can do is to write policy that clearly states that all threats of violence will be taken seriously. Faculty handbooks should require all teachers to report promptly any student threats.

Students who make threats should ordinarily be suspended from the school and be required to receive psychological assessment and counseling. The student can return only if he/she submits a written recommendation for return from a psychologist or psychiatrist and the administration is willing to have the student back on the campus. A second offense should result in automatic removal from the school. Parent/student handbooks do not necessarily have to contain these details, but should indicate that all threats of violence will be taken seriously.

Although adults rarely make such threats, a policy should be in place for all employees and other adult community members that mirrors the student policy, with the exception that, if a threat is verified, the employee is dismissed.

SAMPLE FORMS

A final area that should be included in faculty handbooks involves sample forms. These forms will, of course, differ from school to school. It is certainly practical and efficient to have all forms located in one place. Whatever forms teachers use—report cards, progress reports, deficiency forms, detention slips, accident forms, grade change forms—should be included. Such a procedure ensures that all teachers know what the "official" forms are and have easy access to them.

The components listed above are crucial in faculty handbook development. Other areas may be included and may be important to a given faculty or school.

There is no one right or wrong way to compose a faculty handbook. Each principal has to decide what is important for his or her faculty. The above is simply a discussion of major areas which ought to be included in some way in every faculty handbook. The points discussed should give principals some "food for thought" as they develop or revise handbooks.

The above components are broad areas of concern. More experienced administrators may already have legally sound faculty handbooks in place. As new concerns arise, the administrators will develop policies and rules to meet the new concerns. Sometimes, this kind of reactive approach is unavoidable. Certainly, a proactive approach, which attempts to envision possible difficulties, is preferable to trying to develop policies to meet problems as they arise and after damage has been done.

A sample faculty handbook outline follows. The faculty handbook will generally be lengthier than the parent/student handbook and probably includes most of the material in the parent/student handbook as well as faculty policies and procedures. The following two chapters, which discuss parent/student handbooks and board handbooks, will include checklists but will not include sample outlines.

The outline, which follows, is based on actual handbooks used in Catholic schools. The questions and comments in each section should enable an administrator to focus on items for inclusion in the handbook. After the mission statement, administration of the school and the admissions policy, an alphabetical arrangement of topics is offered, which may be helpful in the initial organization of the handbook.

SAMPLE FACULTY HANDBOOK OUTLINE

Mission, Philosophy and Goals of the School

The mission statement and philosophy of the school should be stated. If there are school goals, these should be included as well. New teachers and veteran ones should be able to quote the mission statement and should use it as a guide in their educational ministry.

Administration of the School

As indicated above, the administrative structure of the school should be outlined. The roles of all persons who are considered administrators should be defined. Teachers should know to whom to go for information and direction. The roles of department heads and levels coordinators should be discussed.

Admission of Students

What is the school's policy on admission? What qualifications must a student possess to be considered for admission? What commitments are expected from students and their parents? The handbook should contain statements of non-discrimination such as, "The school does not discriminate on the basis of race, sex (in a coeducational school), creed, color, or national origin. The school does not discriminate on the basis of disability, if with reasonable accommodations, the student can meet the academic and behavioral requirements of the school." Although admission is primarily an administrative task, it is important that faculty be as well informed as possible since parents and/or students may approach teachers for this type of information.

Academics

What subjects are students required to take? In what subjects must students receive a passing grade in order to be promoted or to graduate? How are grades computed? Some direction with regard to standards is in order. What constitutes "A" work or "unsatisfactory" work?

What is the school or diocesan policy concerning retention of students? If a student is placed in the next grade level because of parental wishes and over the objections of the school's professional staff, how and where is that fact noted? Are parents required to sign a statement that the student is being moved to the next grade against professional advice? Is a different term than "promoted" used in such cases? Students can be "assigned" or "transferred" to the next level.

What responsibilities does a teacher have towards a student who is experiencing academic difficulties? How does a teacher document the fulfillment of these responsibilities?

Accidents

Insurers of Catholic schools have long expressed dismay at the lack of documentation of accidents found in most Catholic schools. Without documentation of an incident, it is difficult for administrators to answer parent claims of student injury after an accident.

What should a teacher do if an accident occurs while supervising students? Should an accident form be automatically filed? Should the principal always be notified? Should the student's parents always be notified? With increasing litigation, the safest course of action is to keep written documentation and notify parents when anything out of the ordinary occurs that could cause student injury.

Activity Record(s)

Student involvement in extra-curricular activities should be documented. What is a teacher's responsibility in this regard? In elementary school, a teacher might keep a card on each student; in junior and senior high school, a homeroom teacher could distribute forms to students and return completed forms to the office.

Announcements

How do teachers receive announcements? Through a bulletin board or through written notices placed in mailboxes? How do teachers make announcements that affect the whole school or students other than those they teach? The answers to these questions can be crucial if an incident should occur and a student or teacher claim that the appropriate announcement was never made.

Assignments

Expectations for homework assignments should be stated. How much homework is given to primary, middle, junior and senior high students? How much time should a teacher expect that students will spend on homework? Should teachers' lesson plan books document assigned homework?

Attendance

What kind of records are homeroom teachers and subject teachers expected to keep? What is the parent responsibility in reporting absence? What procedure should be followed if a teacher discovers that a student whose name is not on the absentee list is actually missing from class? What is the responsibility of teachers regarding make-up work for absent students?

This section should contain a statement that students may never take attendance. Only teachers and professional staff should check attendance. If a student's absence is not properly recorded and some harm should come to the student, both the non-recording teacher and the school could be held responsible for not noting the absence.

The best legal protection for a school in the reporting of student absence is to follow a policy such as this one: "Parents are to call the school before a given time to report a student's absence. If the parent does not call, school personnel will call the parent and/or the person designated by the parent as an emergency contact. Documentation of all such calls and/or attempted calls will be kept."

Boundaries

See above discussion. The administrator may wish to include an article or other information on appropriate professional boundaries.

Child Abuse Laws

The child abuse laws of the state should be included. Policy should underscore the fact that the person who suspects the abuse is the person whose responsibility it is to report the abuse; this responsibility cannot be passed "up" to an administrator. Policy should also advise teachers that they are the reporting agents, not the screening agents, and thus, it is not appropriate for teachers to conduct investigations to determine the truth or falsity of the suspicion. Teachers who make child abuse reports should promptly notify the principal of the fact that a report was made.

Classroom Teachers

All expectations of classroom teachers not otherwise stated in the handbook should be noted in this section.

Close of School Year

What are the professional responsibilities of teachers at the end of a school year? What materials (keys, textbooks, plan books, grade books, etc.) can be kept, and what should be returned to school officials? What, if any, penalties will result from non-compliance?

Confidentiality

See above discussion. Include a directive requiring teachers to tell all students, "I will keep your confidences so long as no one's life, health or safety is at risk."

Corporal Punishment

As protection for the school, faculty handbooks should forbid corporal punishment and should require that, if a teacher does strike a student, the teacher shall promptly report that fact to administrators. Corporal punishment should be defined as, "any touching that can be construed as punitive." Administrators should not prohibit all touching of students, although some public school districts, fearing lawsuits, have issued such prohibitions. Adults should understand what is appropriate behavior. A test might be, "Would I feel all right if I saw a teacher touch my child in the way I touched this child?" Pats on the back, an arm around a tearful child and the like should not be summarily prohibited.

Counseling Services

If the school has a guidance department, its functions should be stated. Procedures for student referral should be included.

Crisis Plans

The school's crisis plan should be found in its entirety. Any special duties of teachers should be noted. All staff and students should participate in crisis drills. A code word or phrase such as, "Mr. Valentine, please come to the office" or "Will the letter carrier please come the office" should alert all to danger. Teachers should require students to lie or sit on the floor while they lock doors and lower blinds or shades.

There should always be designated "safe places" off campus whose owners or managers agree that school members can gather there in the event of an emergency, as it is possible that some students and teachers may be able to escape or be released. The school spokesperson and the process for dealing with media inquiries should also be documented.

Custody Issues

The faculty handbook should contain some discussion of current custody law. Faculty must understand that parents who do not have custody of their children still have rights to access information and to speak with school officials, unless the school has on file a court-certified copy of a court order to the contrary.

Teachers should know how to access information regarding current custody arrangements for their students. Teachers should be cautioned against "taking sides" in custody disputes.

Defamation of Character

Defamation of character can occur when people share damaging information about a third party. There are two kinds of defamation: slander, which is spoken, and libel, which is written. Teachers are generally held to a high standard where communications about students are concerned. Teachers should be cautioned to guard their comments and to make comments about students only to those with a right to know. Written comments should follow these three guidelines: whatever is written should be (1) specific, (2) behaviorally oriented and (3) verifiable.

Department Chairpersons

If a school has department chairpersons, levels coordinators or other administrative personnel, their duties should be noted. Questions that should be answered include, "Do they approve texts? Do they develop curriculum? Do they observe teachers?"

Discipline

The school discipline code should be included in its entirety. Recommendations for constructive and effective discipline might be included here.

Dress Code

If faculty dress code or dress guidelines exist, these should be included. Faculty should be encouraged to dress appropriately as befits professionals who are also role models for younger persons.

Extra-Curricular Activities

The policy concerning faculty members' moderating extra-curricular activities should be stated here, and all moderator responsibilities should be listed. Faculty moderators must understand that they are responsible for the safety of the students and that students cannot be left in the school building or at the activity site without adult supervision.

Faculty Meetings

Are all faculty members required to attend all faculty meetings? Who is responsible for developing the agenda? How does a teacher place an item on the agenda?

Minutes of all meetings should be kept, and each faculty member should receive a copy of the minutes. A copy should be kept on file in the principal's office. It would be advisable to state that faculty members who are excused from attendance at a faculty meeting are responsible for knowing and implementing any decisions made during that meeting.

Family Medical and Leave Act

If the Family Medical and Leave Act applies to the school, its provisions should be listed here. Faculty should be cautioned that they must exhaust all vacation and sick time before FMLA leave can be taken. Generally, FMLA leave is unpaid.

Field Trips

It is now a clearly established part of school law that all field trips must have an educational purpose. If an accident were to occur, a school could much more easily justify an educational trip than one that is purely recreational. If trips to amusement parks, for example, are allowed, teachers should be required to have an educational component as part of the experience.

What permission form is to be used? The following is an example.

I, We, the parent(s)/guardian(s) of _____
request that the school allow my/our son/daughter to participate
in_____.   I, we give permission for
_____'s participation. In consideration for my/our
child's participation, we hereby release, indemnify and save harm-

less the school and its agents from any and all liability for any and all harm that my/our child may sustain as a result of this trip.

The educational purpose of the trip should be included on the form and any special conditions should be noted. For example, if a trip poses some particular risks, such as being near a lake or a wooded area where poisonous plants might be found, those conditions should be noted on the form.

If there is not a standard mode of transportation, such as school buses, the type of transportation for this trip should be noted, and parents should sign that they accept the mode being used. If parents are driving private cars, they should be told whether the school has insurance covering the use of private cars (most schools do not). If the school does not have insurance, parents should be notified of that fact and should understand that they can be held personally liable in the event of accident or injury. Parent volunteer drivers should be asked to furnish a copy of their driver's license and proof of insurance. The same cautions apply when teachers use their own cars. Thus, the use of teacher cars should be discouraged. In no circumstances should teachers be *required* to transport students to off-site trips.

The ratio of children to adult chaperons should be stated. Generally, the rule is that the younger the child is chronologically or mentally, the greater the standard of care.

Procedures for checking forms for forgery should be in place; spot checks are one procedure. The teacher responsible for the trip could be required to check signatures with those that are on file in the office. Perhaps the school secretary could be given the tasks of checking all signatures on field trip forms. When one person consistently checks all forms, the likelihood of finding forgeries increases.

A student who does not have a signed permission form should not be allowed to go on the trip. A phone call from a parent should not be accepted in place of the signed form.

A faxed form from the parent can be accepted.

Fire and other Emergency Drills

Procedures for fire and other emergency drills must be clearly stated, and the responsibilities of teachers must be defined.

Grievance Procedure

If there is a procedure to settle faculty grievances, it should be included here. This procedure may be one developed by the diocese. A matter that is clearly not "grievable" should be identified.

Harassment

See above discussion. Administrators may wish to include a policy statement such as, "Demeaning behavior will not be permitted."

Illness/Leaves of Absence

What should a faculty member do regarding professional duties when ill? Who is notified? If the principal cannot be reached, is there someone else who can be called? Should lesson plans be made available? Are teachers expected to keep a file of student activities that can be used in a teacher's absence?

—Sick Leave

A sick leave policy should answer the following questions:

1. How many days per year may be taken as sick leave?
2. For what reasons may sick leave be taken—spouse or child illness, for example?
3. Does sick leave accumulate?
4. Will a teacher be paid for sick days(s) taken before or after a holiday?
5. May an administrator require a doctor's certificate? When may that be required?

—*Temporary Leaves of Absence*

The same questions as asked regarding sick leave would apply here.

Leaves of absence for personal business, bereavement, armed forces' reserve duty and jury duty should be discussed.

—*Maternity/Paternity Leave*

Is maternity/paternity leave paid or unpaid? How long is it? When should a teacher notify the principal of intent to take leave?

Leaving the School Grounds

May a teacher leave the campus during the school day? If a teacher does leave, what procedures should be followed?

Non-Instructional Duties

Teacher responsibilities for non-instructional duties not otherwise discussed in the handbook could be listed here. Some examples are listed above.

Phone/Parent Conferences

What are the school's expectations regarding conferences with parents in person or by phone? Is a teacher expected to return a parent's phone call within a certain number of hours? What record will the school keep of parent phone calls to teachers? What records of conversations with parents should teachers keep?

Policies of the School

Some faculty handbooks include a separate section for policies not mentioned elsewhere. Expectations regarding teacher participation/presence during assemblies and other activities could also be stated in this section.

Search and Seizure

The United States Supreme Court ruled in *New Jersey v. T.L.O.*, 105 S.Ct. 733 (1985) that public school administrators did not need search warrants or probable cause to search students and their belongings. The Catholic school principal, obviously, is not bound to Fourth Amendment search and seizure requirements either. However, teachers should be given guidelines for any search of student belongings or students. Procedures for searching students should be more stringent than those for searching mere possessions. Whenever possible, a witness should be present during the search. Strip searches should never be permitted.

Student Illness

What procedures should a teacher follow if a student arrives ill, becomes ill in class or during some school activity? Where should such students be sent? Should another student accompany the ill student?

Supervision and Evaluation of Teachers

Who supervises teachers? How often can a teacher expect to be visited? What supervisory format will be followed? Will there be pre and/or post conferences? Will the supervisory instrument become a part of the teacher's file? Are unscheduled classroom visits permitted and/or encouraged? How are teachers evaluated? Teachers should be afforded the right to append their own opinions to supervisory reports and evaluations that become part of personnel files.

Termination of Teachers/Non-Renewal of Contract

If these topics are not discussed elsewhere, they should be included here. What are the procedures for teacher dismissal/non-renewal of contract? Does a teacher have any recourse and, if so, what is it?

The above outline is simply a suggestion of topics that could be included. An administrator should also consider topics that could be pertinent to his or her school. The administrator should commit to developing or revising a faculty handbook according the needs of the school and sound legal principles.

Teacher's Signed Agreement

Teachers should be asked to sign a statement that they have received, read and agree to be governed by the provisions of the faculty handbook.

CHAPTER FIVE
PARENT/STUDENT HANDBOOKS

Catholic school administrators, like all school administra
tors, want to ensure that parents and students understand
the rules of the school and agree to be governed by them.
Administrators should ask parents to discuss the handbook's provisions with their children. Parents share the responsibility for
their children's understanding the mission of the school and the
rules and regulations that flow from that mission. Parents should
be asked to sign a statement that they have read the handbook and
agree to be governed by its provisions. Students may also be
asked to sign similar statements, although they lack the legal
authority to enter into a contract if they are under the age of
eighteen.

When administrators consider handbooks, rules and regulations come to mind. Most school officials and lawyers would
agree that the best school law is, like medicine, preventive. The
best defense is having tried to follow the right course in the first
place. School officials must realize that, despite their best efforts
in any and all areas of school life, they may face lawsuits. All
administrators should carefully construct and examine rules and
procedures in such a way that they are confident that the requirements are reasonable, fair and consistent.

Assuming that the rules of a school have been properly
developed, promulgated and implemented, one must then determine the appropriate procedures to be followed when rules are
violated. Courts assume that school officials are impartial parties
who will give students fair hearings. Decisions in both public and

private school cases insist that fairness is part of the responsibility incumbent upon school personnel as part of the school's contract with students and parents.

Courts look for evidence of good faith. Did the school have a rule that was promulgated to those affected? Did the student know of the rule? The court will not concern itself with the wisdom of the rule—or even with the rightness or wrongness of the professional opinion of the educators. The court is only concerned with the existence of a properly promulgated rule and with the institution's acting in good faith according to its own procedures.

Courts look to the Constitution for guidance in determining whether public school students' rights have been violated. In all school cases, courts look for basic fairness in the execution of the contract existing between the student/parent and the school when the student is alleging that school officials acted improperly in the imposition of disciplinary sanctions.

Administrators must understand that they will never be able to think of every possible student misdeed. Therefore, it is advisable to have some kind of "catch all" clause such as 'other inappropriate conduct." No court will expect a handbook to have contained all possible offense, but courts will expect that *something* is written and that students and parents have a reasonable idea of the expectations of the school. Catholic educators must be concerned with being models of mature, responsible, Christian behavior. Disciplinary policies and procedures must be examined in the light of responsible behavior.

As in the construction of the faculty handbook, the beginning point for development of the parent/student handbook should be the school's mission statement. Every school should have a clearly written mission statement that is available to all members of the school community. Even first graders can understand the mission of the school: "At our school we try to treat each other the way Jesus would." The life of the school should be seen as flowing from the mission of the school.

Rules are just one more manifestation of the school's mission. Rules should be clear and understandable. A test that might be applied by the courts is: would two persons of average intelligence reading this rule have the same understanding of it? A rule stating, "Students arriving at class after the bell has rung will be marked tardy" is clear while a rule such as, "Late students will be marked tardy," is open to such questions as: how late is late? after the bell? after the teacher begins class?

Whenever possible, rules should be written. When emotions run high, it is easier to refer to the written rule than to insist that "at the beginning of the year you were told this." Having a written handbook should encourage the school to strive for clarity in rule making. Periodic evaluation enables the school to make necessary changes.

The checklist which follows may help the administrators judge what is needed in their handbooks and what specific additions, deletions and/or revisions would strengthen the handbook currently in use.

CHECKLIST FOR PARENT/STUDENT HANDBOOKS

What Should a School Have?   *What Does My School Need?*

Mission Statement
Administration
Admission Policies
Academic Policies
Communication
Confidentiality
Counseling Opportunities
    and Expectations
Crisis Plans
Custody Issues
Discipline Code
Extra-curricular Activities
Field Trip Policies/Forms
Medication
Parent Cooperation as Condition
    of Enrollment
Parent Service Requirements
Retreats

What Should a School Have?	*What Does My School Need?*

Student Service Programs
Technology and the Internet
Use of School Grounds
Use of Student Information/
   Pictures
Principal's Right to Amend
Parent(s)' Signed Agreement

MISSION STATEMENT

As stated throughout this text, the mission statement of the school is basic and should be included in all handbooks. Every member of the school community and, indeed, all who come into contact with a school community, should see that persons are striving to live out the mission which guides the school.

If the administrators believe that the mission statement is written in language that is beyond the understanding of the students, an age-appropriate version might be offered.

ADMISSION POLICIES

Non-Discriminatory Statement

As noted earlier, Catholic schools are required to treat all people equally. There can be no discrimination on the basis of race, sex (unless traditionally a single sex school), national origin, age (in accordance with the law), and disability, if, with reasonable accommodation on the part of the school, the disabled person's needs could be met.

Students with Learning Differences

School handbooks should not contain statements such as, "St. Michael's school cannot accommodate special needs." Virtually every Catholic school is accommodating some types of special needs. Section 504 of the Rehabilitation Act of 1973, as amended in 1974, prohibits the arbitrary exclusion of otherwise qualified students if their learning differences can be reasonably accommodated. For perhaps too long, many Catholic school administrators, fearing lawsuits, have focused on why students *cannot* be accommodated. A more appropriate question might be, "What can we do to meet this child's needs?" The school may not have the resources to meet every child's needs, but at least administrators will have made an effort to serve all children.

While seeking to include as many students with learning differences as possible, administrators must guard against making promises that cannot be kept. One way to protect the school legally is to admit every student on a probationary status for a given period of time, perhaps three months; such a provision allows school officials time to determine whether the school can meet the student needs of whatever kind before making acceptance final.

Preference for Catholic Students

Catholic schools may discriminate on the basis of religion, meaning that Catholic schools may give preference to Catholic students. However, if there is an admissions' preference, it should be stated. For example, a policy might state: "This school gives preference in admission first to Catholic students living within the parish boundaries; second, to Catholic students living outside the parish boundaries; third, to non-Catholic students." What is important is that the policy, whatever it is, be clear and documented. Oral policies are hard to enforce.

Financial/Fee Refund Policies

Financial obligations should be clearly stated; if tuition charged, the amount and payment terms should be indicated. Refund policies for entrance fees, tuition, book purchases, and other expenses should be noted. Much ill will can be avoided if parents are told from the very beginning what monies will be refunded.

ACADEMIC POLICIES

Academic Expectations

School administrators expect students to perform to the best of their ability. Many schools require students to have minimally passing grades or to pass a certain number of subjects before being permitted to advance to the next grade and/or to remain in the school.

Students with learning differences pose special issues as discussed above. If standards are different for such students, policy should reflect that reality.

Homework

The school policy concerning homework should be stated here. Parents should know how much time a student at any given grade level ought to spend on homework. The role that the school expects the parents to take in helping with homework should also be clarified.

Grades and Grading

The grading policies of the school should be discussed. Whatever system is used, numerical, letter or other, should be defined. Statements as to what constitutes superior, satisfactory and unsatisfactory work should be given.

In this era when students and parents seem to request grade reconsiderations and recalculations on a somewhat regular basis, administrators would be well-advised to adopt a policy such as, "Any requests for grade changes must be made in writing to the teacher within one week of the receipt of the grade."

Academic Sanctions for Disciplinary Violations

In recent times courts have been extremely reluctant to allow school officials to assign academic penalties for disciplinary violations. A student who is suspended, for example, may be penalized by not being able to make up the work missed, but the student's grade should not be lowered by ten points or one letter grade for the violation. There is a problem even with penalizing for work missed in that a student who is suspended on a day when there are no tests incurs a much less severe penalty than one who is suspended on a day when there are tests. The prudent administrator may wish to consider a prohibition on the use of academic penalties for disciplinary violations and allow suspended students to make up work.

Absence

There is no uniform law about imposing academic penalties for absence. However, recent decisions suggest that courts tend to believe that a student who has demonstrated mastery of content area should be granted credit for that mastery. Thus, administrators should avoid rules that state that students will lose credit after a given number of absences. Some administrators may wish to deny credit for unexcused absences. As administrators know only too well, though, some parents are willing to lie for their children and it becomes difficult to be fair in imposing academic sanctions for absence.

Handbooks should give parents rules for reporting student absence. Parents should be required to telephone the school when a student is going to be absent. When a child is absent and parents have not called, the school should telephone the parents. In the unfortunate and often dangerous situations in which children have been sent to school but never arrive, valuable hours can be lost if the school does not contact the parent about the child's absence.

Disability Issues

As this text is being prepared, Congress is considering a revision of the Individuals with Disabilities in Education Act, so any discussion of disability law here will most likely not reflect the most current law. Therefore, general comments will be made.

As indicated above under "academic standards," schools are not permitted to deny admission arbitrarily. Today there are many kinds of learning disabilities, in addition to physical disabilities. The bottom line is that schools may not discriminate against otherwise qualified individuals on the basis of disability if, with reasonable accommodation, the individual can meet the requirements of the school program.

There is a limit to what schools can be expected to do. The principle of financial exigency guards against institutions being forced to spend so much money on accommodations that the very existence of the institution is at risk. If a student needs elevator access and installing an elevator would bankrupt the school or parish, the accommodation would be considered unreasonable. Similarly, the school would not be expected to hire a full-time sign language interpreter for a student. Some Catholic schools permit such accommodations, but require the parents to pay for the services.

It must be frankly stated, however, that simply because one is not legally required to do something, it does not follow that one should not do that thing, if it is the *right* action to take. If a school has significant assets and could afford a sign language interpreter for a deaf student or instructions in signing for the faculty and staff, the principal may have a moral and ethical duty to provide for the student even though the law does not require such provision. Indeed, the *Pastoral Statement of U.S. Catholic Bishops on Handicapped People* (1978) seems to demand such action: "If handicapped people are to become equal partners in the Christian community, injustices must be eliminated." Certainly Catholic schools should be leaders in remedying injustice wherever it is found, especially as it affects those whose disabilities require special accommodations in Catholic schools.

Students with learning differences are children of God and members of the Church. The challenge is to find resources to meet the learning differences of students within our Catholic schools. Many schools now have a staff member who has responsibilities for students with learning differences. As more and more disabilities and differences are identified, the challenges will increase.

Promotion/Retention

Promotion and retention policies should be outlined. Many dioceses have guidelines concerning reasons for which a student may be retained in a grade. If the diocese or school permits a student's entering the next grade simply because a parent wishes the child to be in the next grade, the documentation that will be kept should be noted. In any event, when a student is transferred over the advice of the professional staff, parents should be required to sign a statement that they realize that the transfer is against the professional advice of the staff. Such documentation can protect the school if later allegations are made that the student should not have been placed in the next grade. Students who have not achieved sufficient mastery of curricula should not be promoted to the next grade, but rather should be assigned or transferred. Promoting students who have not mastered curricula can leave the school open for liability for malpractice.

Records Prior to 1975, parents and students did not have any legal rights to see school records. In 1975, the Buckley Amendment gave parents and students over the age of fourteen the right of access to records and the right to request that statements be changed or deleted. If school officials refuse to change or delete records, statements made by parents or students must be included in the record. Although no Supreme Court case involving Catholic schools and rights of access to records has been brought by parents or students, Catholic school administrators would be well advised to follow the regulations in the Buckley Amendment. It is generally prudent to avoid actions that could result in litigation.

The school handbook should state what procedures are to be followed if a parent or student wishes to view a record. The school can ask for twenty-four hours' notice and can require the parent to make the request in writing.

One way that any school can safeguard itself against legal problems in the area of records is to limit what is kept in official files. The following are all that are required: academic transcripts, academic testing, health records (unless kept in a health office), and an emergency sheet. Any other records, particularly disciplinary ones, can and should be kept elsewhere. The parent/student handbook should inform parents of the types of documents that are placed in student files. School officials must understand,

and may wish to note in handbooks, that only the contents of the official file will be forwarded to a new school.

COMMUNICATION

Many problems can be avoided if the school handbook contains the procedures by which parents contact school officials and school officials contact parents.

Complaints and the Principle of Subsidiarity

In keeping with church principles of subsidiarity, problems should be solved at the lowest level whenever possible. Thus, persons having a problem with a teacher would go directly to that teacher before going to the assistant principal or principal. If a parent is reluctant to confront a teacher alone, the administrator might offer to be present at a conference. Requiring persons to attempt to work out their difficulties mutually is certainly consistent with the demands of the Gospel and makes good legal sense as well. Handbooks might contain a policy statement such as, "Complaints should be handled at the lowest possible level. Persons with concerns about a teacher should first attempt to address the concern with the teacher. Only after such attempts have failed, should administrators be contacted."

Other Communication

If a parent wishes to communicate with a teacher, how should contact be made? Spontaneous visits to classrooms ought to be discouraged, but a parent could be directed to make an appointment. If the teacher wishes to contact the parent, how might the parent expect that the contact will be made? Parents need this information.

How should a parent contact an administrator? If an appointment is necessary, how should it be made? Obviously, there are many times when informal contacts will occur. There are also times when everyone will profit if people have an opportunity to distance themselves from a situation before discussing it. Thus, the existence of a procedure for communication can be helpful.

CONFIDENTIALITY

As indicated in the preceding chapter, confidentiality is a topic that merits special consideration. Parents expect that school officials will give them necessary information concerning the health, life and safety of their children.

Confidentiality is generally held to mean that one individual or individuals will keep private information that has been given to them, and will not reveal it. For example, the person who receives the sacrament of reconciliation rightfully expects that the subject matter of confession will be held sacred by the confessor and will not be revealed to anyone. Students expect that teachers and other staff members will keep confidences. But, if a student tells a teacher that he or she is going to harm self or others, the teacher must reveal that information even if a promise of confidentiality has been given. As discussed earlier, a number of parents have filed lawsuits against teachers and school districts when teachers knew of a student's wish to harm self or others and failed to report it. This failure represents a new type of negligence, failure to warn.

It is a widely held myth that counselors, physicians and social workers have legal immunity from responsibility for any injuries that may arise from their not acting on confidential information presented to them. A counselor who hears from a young person that the individual plans to kill his or her parents and does nothing about it will not be legally able to decline to answer questions under oath, nor will the counselor be held harmless for any resulting injuries if he or she decides not to reveal the threats. Counselors and teachers must make it very clear to confiding individuals that they will keep their confidences unless health, life or safety or those of another are involved.

Administrators may wish to include a policy statement such as, "Teachers will keep confidential information entrusted to them so long as no one's life, health or safety is at stake. Parents will be promptly notified of teacher concerns."

COUNSELING OPPORTUNITIES AND EXPECTATIONS

Counselors used to be found primarily in high schools. Today, elementary schools often have counselors on staff or provide access to counseling services. The handbook should identify counseling services and procedures for accessing them. Conflicts can arise when parents do not wish their children to be seen by a counselor. A simple policy statement such as, "Counselors may see a student for up to three times without parental notification and consent. After the third visit, parents will be notified. If serious concerns exist, parents will be promptly notified whenever the concerns arise."

CRISIS PLANS

The development of crisis plans is beyond the scope of this text. Various NCEA resources can provide guidance for those who seek help in the construction of such plans. Every school should have a crisis plan and the parts of it that affect parents and students should be included in the handbook. At the very least, parents should be told which television and radio channels should be consulted for information. The handbook should also identify "safe places" to which students will be brought, and from which parents can claim them, in the event the crisis requires evacuation of the building.

CUSTODY

Schools must have accurate custodial information on file. Non-custodial parents do have rights. The law protects non-custodial parents and maintains that parents do not cease to be parents when they no longer have custody of their children. Therefore, handbooks may include a statement such as:

This school abides by the provisions of the Buckley Amendment with respect to the rights of non-custodial parents. In the absence of a court order to the contrary, a school will provide the non-custodial parent with access to academic records and other school information regarding his or her child. If there is a court order specifying that there is to be no information given, it is the custodial parent's responsibility to provide the school with an a court-certified copy of the court order.

Another way to handle the non-custodial parent situation is to ask all divorced parents to furnish the school with a court-certified copy of the custody section of the divorce decree. Never married parents should also have custody documents on file, as needed. This information will help school officials in determining when, if ever, the child can be released to the non-custodial parent.

DISCIPLINE CODE

Respect for the Dignity of All

Perhaps the most important factor to consider in the development of a discipline code is respect for the dignity of all. Virtually every rule and regulation should be grounded in this respect. Students and faculty should understand that one of their first obligations in a Catholic school is to respect the dignity of all members of the school community.

General Guidelines

School administrators should strive for simplicity and clarity in rule construction; long lists of rules should probably be avoided. Phrases such as "other inappropriate behavior" or "conduct unbecoming a student in a Catholic school" cover many types of misbehavior. Examples of infractions could be provided.

The administration should retain the right to make exceptions to existing rules and regulations. There may be a case in which mitigating circumstances call for a different response than has been the norm in the past. A phrase such as, "the principal is the final recourse in all disciplinary situations and may waive any disciplinary rule for just cause at his or her discretion" may be in order. While this may appear to be inviting persons to seek exceptions, it avoids the risk of "boxing" one's self into a corner with rules that offer no flexibility. Phrases such as "must" or "will" result in a certain penalty leave little leeway. Phrases such as "can" or "may" give an administrator room to allow for individual circumstances.

Harassment

Harassment regulations need to be grounded in the belief that all persons have a right to be treated with dignity. All demeaning behavior should be prohibited.

Sexual harassment is an area of increasing concern. One definition for sexual harassment might be "conduct, containing sexual suggestions, that would be offensive to a reasonable person." Principals will want to place any regulations in age-appropriate terms. According to federal law, sexual harassment includes but is no limited to:

(1) verbal conduct such as epithets, derogatory jokes or comments, slurs or unwanted sexual advances, imitations or comments;

(2) visual contact such as derogatory and/or sexually oriented posters, photography, cartoons, drawings or gestures;

(3) physical contact such as assault, unwanted touching, blocking normal movements or interfering with work, study or play because of some sexual matter;

(4) threats and demands to submit to sexual requests for certain benefits; and

(5) retaliation for having reported or threatened to report sexual harassment.

The following are some specific examples of behaviors that could constitute sexual harassment: sexual propositions, off-color jokes, inappropriate physical contact, innuendos, sexual offers, looks and gestures. In a number of recent public school cases, female students alleged that male students made sexual statements to them and that school officials, after being informed, declined to take action and stated that "boys will be boys."

Female students have generally prevailed in such cases.

Although one can argue that the person who sexually harasses another should be liable and not the school and its administrators, case law is suggesting that administrators who ignore such behavior or do not take it seriously can be held liable for the behavior. Thus, clear statements in handbooks can help provide evidence that administrators act in appropriate ways.

Procedures for reporting sexual harassment should then be given. If there is a diocesan policy in effect, it may be printed in its entirely, perhaps in an appendix, or it can be referenced. Procedures should include a statement such as, "All allegations of sexual harassment will be taken seriously and promptly investigated." Confidentiality should be stressed. Concern should be expressed for both the alleged victim and the alleged perpetrator. Any forms that are to be used can be included.

It is far easier to prevent claims of sexual harassment than it is to defend them.

Administrators may wish to consider having programs concerning harassment and right treatment of people as part of the school's curriculum.

Violence—Threatened and Acted

School handbooks must state that all threats of violence will be taken seriously. The term "zero tolerance" is in vogue today. Administrators must be sure that they understand what they mean by that term and are able to translate that meaning into understandable terms in the parent/student handbook. Some educators believe that zero tolerance means that any violence, threatened or acted, will result in dismissal from school. Such an approach can be problematic, however. If a first grader tells another first grader who took his toy, "I'm going to kill you," it hardly seems just to dismiss the student from school. More age-appropriate remedies might be in order. Clearly, once an administrator believes that the presence of a student in the school poses a safety threat for others in the school, the student must be removed from the school setting.

The safety of everyone must be the predominant concern of every administrator. At the same time, all students—even those who threaten or do violence—must be treated with dignity.

Conduct, Whether Inside or Outside the School

Students engage in behaviors outside the school that reflect poorly on the school and/or suggest that the student may pose a danger in the school. In the past, it was not unusual to hear parents protesting that whatever their children did, it took place outside school and was not the business of the school. A "catch all clause" can provide the school with the protection it needs. One example of such a clause would be, "The student is a St. Joan's student at all times. A student who engages in conduct, whether inside or outside the school, that is detrimental to the reputation of the school, may be disciplined by school officials."

Due Process/Appeals

While considering the development of procedural due process guidelines, administrators should be aware that there is a time investment involved. If a teacher allows a student to tell his or her side of a story instead of summarily imposing punishment, the teacher makes a commitment to spending time with a student who faces discipline. The principal or disciplinarian makes a commitment to listening to the student's side of the story as well as to the teacher's, and the benefit should be obvious: students perceive teachers and administrators as trying to be fair and, one hopes, will internalize the values thus modeled.

All Catholic school personnel, then, should commit themselves to notice and a hearing in any disciplinary situation; in this way, the school meets the minimum requirements of Christian due process and commonly accepted standards of good faith and fair dealing. This commitment would mean that the student is told what he or she did that was wrong and is given a chance to be heard.

Somewhat more extensive procedures should be developed if the penalty is suspension. One-day suspensions, at minimum, should require that the principal be involved and that the parents be notified. Longer suspensions should involve the same notification but should also include a written notice of the charges and an indication of the time and place of the hearing. Cases in which the possibility of expulsion exists require more formal notification and a hearing at which the student should normally be able to confront accusers. Careful documentation should be kept.

Public schools must grant a student facing expulsion the right to bring legal counsel to the hearing. Catholic school personnel, however, should avoid the presence of legal counsel. To allow a student to bring an attorney could be setting a precedent. The presence of attorneys often results in adversarial situations which can make the achievement of any sort of pastoral reconciliation very difficult.

This discussion of discipline should be helpful to Catholic school administrators as they attempt to develop and modify rules and policies. The guiding principle in any discussion of discipline and due process should be the desire to act in a Christian manner characterized by fairness and compassion.

A Related Topic: Maternity/Paternity Policies

Catholic schools, elementary as well as secondary, face the situation of unwed mothers and fathers. In the not too distant past, this topic was considered a disciplinary one, and it was not unusual to see unwed mothers removed from school attendance. The issue is certainly an emotionally charged one. The reality is, however, that some students and their parents will consider abortion as an alternative, if school sanctions are too severe. Is a real, if unintended, message being sent that abortion is an answer that will help the student to save face and continue in the Catholic school? As members of a church committed to the preservation of life at all levels, the Catholic school administrator must act in ways consistent with that commitment. At the very least, students should be allowed to finish their work and receive grades and diplomas. The vast majority of Catholic high schools permit unwed parents to remain in attendance. The situation is perhaps more problematic in the grade school, but no less worthy of compassion. Handbooks should contain a statement such as, "Pregnancy is not a reason for dismissal from school." To do otherwise seems to indicate an unwillingness to support a student who has made a choice to give life, rather than to end it.

EXTRA-CURRICULAR ACTIVITIES

All extra-curricular activities sponsored by the Catholic school should be listed, along with the requirements for participation. If certain academic and conduct standards must be maintained for participation, these should be noted.

Any other policies that may be in effect should also be noted. If, for example, a student must be in school in order to participate in a sport or other activity on a given day, that fact should be clarified. As far as possible, the same standards for all extra-curricular activities should be set and maintained. It does not seem fair for a basketball player to be denied participation in her sport because of low grades, if a drama club member with similar academic standing can continue in the club simply because state or diocesan standards govern only participation in athletics.

FIELD TRIP POLICIES/FORMS

Privilege Not a Right
Field trips are privileges given to students; no student has an absolute right to a field trip. The school handbook should state that field trips are privileges and that students can be denied participation if they fail to meet academic and/or behavioral requirements.

Standard Permission Form
It is an excellent practice to include a copy of the school or diocesan permission form in the handbook. Then, if a student forgets to bring the form home, a parent can copy the proper form from the book and fill in the appropriate date and destination. School officials should not accept forms other than the official one. Letters stating, "Mary can go with you today," simply provide no legal protection for the school.

The handbook should state that students who fail to submit

a proper form will not be allowed to participate in the filed trip. The handbook should also state that telephone calls will not be accepted in lieu of written permission. Faxed permission forms can be accepted. The right of parents to refuse to allow their child to participate in a field trip might also be mentioned.

Liability of the School

Although no parent can sign away a child's right to safety, a handbook should state that the parents are expected to sign the permission form which releases the school from liability. Administrators must understand, of course, that there is no such protection from the consequences of negligent behavior on the part of school staff; however, a proper form offers a school as much protection as can be had and serves as a bargaining tool for settlement in the case of litigation.

MEDICATION

Students routinely arrive at school with medication that their parents expect the school to dispense to them. Few schools have nurses on their staffs. Whether a school has a nurse or does not have one, administrators must grapple with appropriate policies and procedures. Some approaches include: (1) all medication must be brought to the office with a parent's note of authorization; (2) only prescription medication can be brought to school and must be stored in a school office; no over-the-counter medication allowed, unless a doctor's written authorization is submitted; (3) prescription medication must be in the original bottle with the student's name on it and written parental permission submitted; (4) the school will not dispense medication, so students are responsible for their own medication; (5) the school does not dispense over-the-counter medication so a parent must come to school to administer the medication; or (6) some variation of these positions.

Opinions vary as to the best approach. Some medical professionals do not want to write notes for over-the-counter medications. Parents grumble about an extra trip to the doctor's to get written authorization. Some high schools expect students to be responsible for self-administering all medication.

The practice of schools storing parent supplied over-the-counter medication appears to be growing. Even though written permission was on file, principals have been sued for administering parent-supplied medication which interacted with some other medicine the student was taking. Some parents allege that school officials should have recognized the possibility of drug interaction and should have asked questions concerning other medications. Several cases of this type are currently in the court system.

The following statements offer some suggestions to ponder when medication policies and procedures are being determined.

(1) The only students who have an absolute right to the administration of medication are those who have serious chronic and/or life-threatening illnesses.

(2) Persons (at least two) must be identified who will be trained in the administration of injections or other drugs that a student cannot self-administer.

(3) Students must be allowed to carry medication for life threatening attacks. Asthma is one such condition that may give no warning; if an inhaler is not immediately available, the student could be severely harmed.

(4) Adults who administer medication must place their whole attention on the task.

(5) If a teacher has a student with a life threatening illness, the teacher must learn how to administer the medication. This reality is a matter of law, not choice.

(6) Young children should not be responsible for oral medication, other than inhalers. Oral medication should be kept in the office.

(7) High school students may be allowed to carry and monitor their own medication, so long as the parent/ student handbook contains a statement to that effect.

PARENT COOPERATION AS A CONDITION OF ENROLLMENT

Today it is not uncommon for principals to ask how to "get rid" of a parent who is disrupting the school environment, will not comply with school rules and regulations, and/or refuses to accept the authority of school officials. Contract law governs Catholic schools and the courts have indicated that they will not compel performance of a contract if one person no longer wishes to be in a private contractual relationship. Understanding that requiring a parent to withdraw a child should be a last resort, school administrators may wish to include a statement such as, "The education of a student is a partnership between the parents and the school. Just as the parent has the right to withdraw a child if desired, the school administration reserves the right to require the withdrawal of a student if the administration determines that the partnership is irretrievably broken." In such instances, it is wise to refund any tuition paid for the year, as the measure of damages for breach of contract would generally be the amount of money paid.

PARENT SERVICE REQUIREMENT

Definition

Many Catholic school administrators find that they cannot operate their schools without support beyond that provided by tuition. It is perfectly legitimate to require parents to give some sort of service in addition to the payment of tuition. However, parents must be informed of this requirement when enrolling their children; thus, the handbook should contain the policy.

The handbook should define what is expected. Is the parent required to give a certain number of hours of service to the school? What sorts of activities meet these requirements? Is the parent or student expected to participate in fundraising? Is there any alternative? For example, can a parent pay an additional fee and thus avoid service? What is the penalty for non-participation?

PARENT ORGANIZATIONS

The names and functions of all school or school-related organizations to which parents may belong should be listed, along with the requirements for participation. The role of the school board or advisory committee, if there is one, should be defined and the method for making contact with the board and/or attending meetings should be noted.

STUDENT RETREATS

Once found only in high schools, elementary schools now may offer retreat programs to students. Occasionally, a parent may not wish his or her child to participate. School officials have the right to require student participation in retreats. The school policy should be stated along with the procedures for requesting that a student not participate.

STUDENT SERVICE PROGRAMS

The majority of Catholic schools have student service programs of some type. The philosophy and expectations of the program should be noted. The United States Supreme Court has upheld student service programs in public schools, so there should be no argument concerning whether Catholic schools can require them. The handbook should state that participation in the service program is a requirement for graduation. Since parents should sign the handbook and thus indicate their acceptance of its contents, there should be little debate over a student's participation.

TECHNOLOGY AND THE INTERNET

Technology now makes available services for students that were previously unimagined. School handbooks should discuss the right use of technology.

Every school should have an Internet Usage Policy which

regulates student use of the Internet and outlines appropriate behaviors. Students must be responsible for accessing only appropriate web sites and reporting any accidental "hits" of inappropriate sites. Forbidden behaviors should be listed.

The Diocese of Rochester, New York, Department of Catholic Schools: *Guidelines and Policies* lists the following as unacceptable behaviors:

- Sending, displaying, or downloading offensive messages or pictures;
- Using obscene language;
- Harassing, insulting, or threatening others
- Damaging of computer systems or computer networks;
- Violating copyright laws;
- Submitting documents from the Internet as a student's personal work;
- Using another person's sign-on and/or password;
- Trespassing in someone else's folder, work, or files;
- Intentionally wasting limited resources;
- Using the network for commercial purposes;
- Revealing a personal phone number, name or address of one's self or another.

These prohibited behaviors may prove helpful to persons writing usage policies for the first time. Students who do not comply with usage rules should forfeit their usage privileges.

USE OF SCHOOL GROUNDS

Case law indicates that schools can be held responsible for accidents on playgrounds or other school property before or after school. Some schools have a policy stating that children are not to arrive before a specified time and are to leave by a certain hour. But it is a policy or rule that is often not enforced. No administrator wants to be insensitive to the problems of working parents; however, it is not fair for parents to assume that it is permissible to drop children at school very early in the morning and/or to pick them up very late in the afternoon. It is also not fair to assume that teachers or administrators who arrive at school early or stay late will be responsible for children. If a child is injured while on school property during an unsupervised time, a court will look to the parent/student handbook to see if a policy is in place, and if it has been enforced.

Athletic practices and other activities, such as parish-sponsored programs, pose problems as well. The question of supervision must be addressed in the handbook and parents must know what the school will and will not do. The law is well-established that schools can be held liable for student injury occurring at unsupervised times, particularly if the school had no policy or failed to enforce the one it had.

There are several approaches to this supervision problem and only the administrators of each school can determine what might work for their situation. One is to post "no trespassing" signs and enforce a policy of no student presence on school grounds outside specified times. If a student is on the grounds at a time when no supervision is provided, the parents should be notified. Appropriate warnings and penalties should be given. Administrators, pastors, and board members may want to consider policy that would require parents to withdraw a child from school after repeated offenses.

Another approach would be to provide funds to pay someone to supervise before and after school, particularly at the elementary level. With more schools adding extended care programs, another solution is possible. A policy might state that any child who is present in the school building or grounds at proscribed times will be placed in extended care and the parents will be billed for the service. High school supervision is somewhat more complex, but administrators must ensure that someone with authority is present at all times when students are on campus.

There are, of course, other options. It is, however, important to take some action. Administrators should not take refuge in the mistaken belief that because nothing has ever happened, nothing ever will. One lawsuit could be extremely costly and could perhaps be avoided if rules, policies and procedures had been developed and enforced.

USE OF STUDENT INFORMATION/ PICTURES

A common question, particularly in the light of school web pages, is whether the school has the right to use student pictures on the web or in other publications? Generally, the law allows for the release of directory information, *i.e.* names and addresses, to appropriate persons. However, addresses should not be posted on websites or referenced in print materials for reasons of safety and privacy.

Administrators may wish to include a policy such as, "The school reserves the right to use student pictures in publications and on the school's website. Any parent who does not wish his or her child's picture used must notify the principal in writing prior to the beginning of the school year."

SCHOOL/PRINCIPAL'S RIGHT TO AMEND HANDBOOK

Administrators should include a clause stating that the school or the principal retains the right to amend the handbook for just cause and that parents will be given prompt notification if changes are made.

SIGNED PARENTAL AGREEMENT

For everyone's protection, parents should be required to sign a statement such as, "We have read and agree to be governed by this handbook." Such a statement avoids many of the problems that can arise when parents or students state that they did not know a given rule existed. Students may also be required to sign an agreement, but their signatures will not be legally binding.

School officials would be well advised to admit a student

to classes only when a signed agreement is submitted. Since courts construe handbooks as part of the contract existing between the school and the parents, it is both legally and ethically wise to ensure that parents have read the handbook and agree to be governed by its provisions.

Conclusion

Writing a handbook is an art, but it is an art that can be learned. Once a school has a sound handbook, it is relatively easy to keep the book updated. Each school is unique and so there will be other policies and procedures than the ones mentioned here included.

CHAPTER SIX—
BOARD HANDBOOKS

C atholic school boards, advisory councils and commissions are now an established part of Catholic school operations. Administrators should find boards to be a source of strength and support. The relationships between and among pastors, principals and board members should be mutually beneficial. In order for boards, pastor and principals to achieve maximum good, it is important that the role of the board be carefully delineated and the scope of its authority defined. Board members have a right to expect that they will be given the information and documents which they need in order to perform their tasks effectively.

Board members must understand that their only real power is vested in the board acting as a board. Individual board members have no actual power and should guard against receiving complaints from parents and teachers that should be brought to appropriate administrators instead of to board members.

Principals are often asked to provide board members with pertinent information. Sometimes, principals are expected to compile a handbook for board members. Since a board handbook will include documents already discussed in this text, faculty handbooks and parent/student handbooks, this chapter will briefly consider other elements that should be present in board handbooks.

Canon, or Church law, governs Catholic schools. Catholic schools and board members have no authority to act outside the provisions of canon law. Within those provisions, however, Catholic schools have great freedom so long as no civil laws are broken. Catholic school boards have much wider latitude in the development of policies and rules than do their public school counterparts.

The following checklist may be helpful to school administrators in developing or revising a board handbook or manual.

BOARD HANDBOOK CHECKLIST

What Should My School
Have Concerning?   *What Does My School Need?*

Mission Statement
By-laws/Constitutions
Role of the Board
Policies
Meetings
Minutes
Financial Information
Confidentiality
Special Issues

MISSION STATEMENT

It is crucial that board members understand and "own" the mission statement of the school. Board members probably have less day-to-day contact with the lived experience of the school than do faculty, students, administrators and parents. Thus it is essential that board members be thoroughly familiar with the mission statement and be able to make decisions and/or recommendations in light of it.

BY-LAWS/CONSTITUTIONS

Written by Persons with Authority

Every school board or council should have by-laws and/or constitutions. Some dioceses provide parishes with such documents and each board is expected to follow the same general format. In the case of private schools or schools owned by religious congregations, the appropriate supervisory party should supply the necessary documents.

Adopted/Accepted by the Board

According to the by-laws and/or constitutions, the board members should adopt or accept the governance document. Board members should receive a thorough orientation to the mission statement and the governance document before beginning membership on the board or as soon as possible thereafter.

Appropriate Components

1. Scope of Authority

There are five types of schools in our Catholic system: parish, inter-parish, diocesan, private and those owned by religious congregations. There are two main types of board structures: advisory or consultative and boards with limited jurisdiction.

An advisory or consultative board is one generally established by the pastor or principal or by diocesan policy. This board has responsibilities for the development and/or recommendation of policies. The pastor or other administrator has the final authority to accept or reject the board's recommendations.

A board with limited jurisdiction has more autonomy in certain decision-making areas than does the consultative board because certain powers have been delegated to its members. Pastors, bishops and religious superiors can delegate power, but they cannot delegate their ultimate responsibilities for actions taken in their parish or diocese or school.

Private schools, including both those owned by religious congregations and those owned by boards of trustees, may have either advisory boards or boards with limited jurisdiction.

2. Role of the Board

The school board has specific responsibilities to the diocese and/or parish and/or sponsoring congregation or entity. The school board must ensure that its policies are consistent with those of the diocese or sponsoring entity. Even private Catholic schools not owned by the diocese are subject to the bishop in matters of faith and morals and may not call themselves "Catholic schools" without his approval.

Faith and Morals

As this text has indicated, cases involving faith and morals can be very complex. Diocesan policy may state that only Catholics who actively practice their religion in accordance with the teachings on the Church may be hired and retained in schools owned and operated by the diocese or parishes within the diocese. But who defines what being a practicing Catholic means? The situation of the divorced Catholic contracting a second marriage without an annulment of the first marriage is perhaps the one most often faced by Catholic school administrators. Even if the person in question is convinced that he or she is acting in good conscience in contracting such a marriage, there is little doubt that the person is, objectively speaking, a probable source of scandal. This situation is not a problem from the standpoint of terminating the employment of a person who violates Church law, but there are cases in which teachers have sued Catholic schools after being dismissed for contracting such marriages. The courts have generally supported the school's right to hold its employees to Church teachings and to dismiss those who act at variance with them, so long as administrators act within established policy. The problem is the lack of consistency from diocese to diocese, from school to school and even within the same school.

Termination Issues

A board will not make the decision to terminate a teacher's employment, as that is an administrative decision, but since the board suggests and/or approves policy, it must support a decision that is based on policy. If the board functions as a review board, its role is to review any case brought to it on appeal to see that basic fairness has been met and that the school or principal has followed appropriate policies; its role is not to decide whether members would have made the same decision or to substitute its judgment for that of the school administrators.

A word of caution is in order. The policies and procedures governing termination and/or non-renewal of contract must be clearly written and understood by all those affected. If staff members can be eliminated, for example, because of the need to reduce employees, this policy should be stated as should the process by which it is implemented. If appointment to certain positions is dependent on board approval, as is sometimes the case in the initial appointment of principals, that fact should be stated.

School boards have responsibilities to the principal. The principal is, in a very real sense, the board's chief executive officer. One way that the board can support the principal is by annually reviewing the school handbooks to be sure they are consistent with policy and should then accept them as a matter of record. Such review and acceptance strengthens the authority of the principal and ensures that the rights and responsibilities of all members of the school community are respected.

3. Membership

By-laws, constitutions or resolutions should state minimum and maximum numbers of board members. In the case of a school owned or sponsored by a religious community, there may be a requirement that a certain percentage of the board be members of the religious community. Some boards reserve a certain number of places for parents of students in the school; others take the position that it can be a conflict of interest for parents of current students to serve and do not generally have parents on the board. Any such requirements should be defined.

It is most important that length of terms be a matter of policy. Boards that do not require persons to "rotate off" can find that there is little or no "new blood," and the structure can become somewhat inflexible. The best model might be one that would call for two terms of two or thee years each, after which a member would have to "retire" for at least a year.

The methods of nominating and electing members should be determined and made available to all interested persons. The titles and responsibilities of board officers should be a matter of policy, as well as the process for electing officers. Standing committees should be named and their functions described. Any annual or other meeting requirements should be clearly a matter of record.

POLICIES

Board function must be understood in terms of policy, a term generally defined as a guide for discretionary action. Policy will dictate what is to be done, but not with how it is done. Policy is not concerned with administration or implementation. Thus, the board should not become involved in how its directives will be implemented or with the specific persons who will implement them. For example, policy might require that students wear uniforms. The board would not be concerned with what company provides the uniforms or with what color they are. Such questions are administrative ones and the principal should deal with them. Administrative decisions are the day-to-day management choices of the principal. It is important that everyone understand these distinctions. Generally, boards will set policies in such areas as: administration, personnel, plant, curriculum, and finances, among others.

The board should ensure that the administration is implementing policies and should expect regular reports. The board may have some responsibility in evaluating the principal's job performance, at least in relationship to the board.

Personnel policies concerning hiring and dismissal procedures, as well as grievance procedures, are the province of the board. As stated earlier, the board should not be concerned with *who* is hired and *who* is dismissed, but rather that hiring and termination are conducted according to policy. If the board functions at any level as part of an appeals process, members should understand that they are to determine whether policies and procedures were fairly followed, not whether a different decision should have been made.

If a parish council or other body does not have responsibility for the school plant, the board may have that duty. The board must ensure that building safety is a priority and that all civil codes are met. The board should ensure that an annual safety audit is conducted and a safety plan kept current. Board members should review school crisis plans and offer suggestions, as appropriate.

MINUTES

Formal minutes of all board and committee meetings should be kept. Board members should be responsible for filing these minutes and keeping them in good order.

FINANCIAL INFORMATION

Whatever financial information is needed by board members should be available to them. Depending on the board's degree of responsibility for finances, budgets and audits should be made available.

CONFIDENTIALITY

Board members have a sacred responsibility to keep the confidences they receive in their capacities as board members. This responsibility should be stressed in orientation and from time to time so that no board member loses sight of this trust.

SPECIAL TOPICS

In these days of increasing litigation, board members should be especially aware of legal developments concerning harassment, child abuse and violence. Chapters Three and Four deal with these topics in detail and should be consulted for further information.

A Concluding Thought

Jesus said, "Render unto Caesar the things that are Caesar's and unto God the things that are God's." The author hopes that this text serves as a bridge between legal requirements and Gospel mandates.

GLOSSARY OF TERMS

BOARD: a board (committee/council/commission) is a body whose members are selected or elected to participate in decision-making in education at the diocesan, regional, inter-parish or parish level.

Board with Limited Jurisdiction: A board with limited jurisdiction has power limited to certain areas of educational concern. It has final but not total jurisdiction.

Consultative or Advisory Board: A consultative board is one which recommends policy.

COLLEGIALITY: Collegiality is a sharing of responsibility and authority. In the Catholic Church, bishops have the highest authority within a diocese. Powers may be delegated to other parties, such as boards.

COMMON LAW: Common law is that law not created by a legislature. It includes principles of action based on long-established standards of reasonable conduct and on court judgments affirming such standards. It is sometimes called "judge-made law."

COMPELLING STATE INTEREST: Compelling state interest is the overwhelming or serious need for governmental action. The government is said to have a compelling state interest in anti-discrimination legislation or the equal treatment of all citizens.

CONTRACT: A contract is an agreement between two parties. The essentials of a contract are: (1) mutual assent (2) by legally competent parties (3) for consideration (4) to subject matter that is legal and (5) in a form of agreement that is legal.

DEFAMATION: Defamation is communication that injures the reputation of another without good reason. Defamation can be either spoken (slander) or written (libel).

DUE PROCESS: Due process is fundamental fairness under the law. There are two types: substantive (what is the "substance" of which a person will be deprived?) and procedural (what process is due and will be used?)

FIDUCIARY: A fiduciary is one who has accepted the responsibility for thecare of people or property.

FORESEEABILITY: Foreseeability is the reasonable anticipation that harm or injury may result from one's action or inaction. It is not necessary that a person anticipate that a specific injury might result from an action, but only that danger or harm in general might result.

JUDICIAL RESTRAINT: Judicial restraint is the doctrine that courts will not interfere in decisions made by professionals.

LANDMARK COURT DECISIONS: Landmark court decisions are decisions of major importance. These decisions are often used as part of the judicial reasoning in later decisions.

NEGLIGENCE: Negligence is the absence of the degree of care which a reasonable person would be expected to use in a given situation.

POLICY: A policy is a guide for discretionary action. Policy states *what* is to be done, not *how* it is to be done.

PROXIMATE CAUSE: Proximate cause is a contributing factor to an injury. The injury was a result or reasonably foreseeable outcome of the action or inaction said to be the proximate cause.

PUBLIC BENEFIT THEORY: The theory which states that an institution which performs a public benefit is a state agent. This theory has been generally rejected by the courts.

STATE ACTION: State action is the presence of the government in an activity to such a degree that the activity may be considered to be that of the government.

SUBSIDIARITY: Subsidiarity is the principle that problems should be solved at the lowest possible level. Thus, if there is a complaint against a teacher, the teacher must be confronted before the principal is approached.

TENURE: Tenure is an expectation of continuing employment.

De Facto Tenure: *De facto* tenure is an expectation in fact that employment will continue, in the absence of a formal tenure policy. *De facto* tenure can result from past practices of an employer or from length of employment.

BIBLIOGRAPHY

Black, Henry Campbell. *Black's law dictionary.* (6th ed.). St. Paul: West, 1990.

Bob Jones University v. United States 103 S. Ct. 2017 (1983).

Bright v. Isenbarger 314 F. Supp. 1382 (1970).

Dixon v. Alabama State B.O.E. 294 F. 2d 150, cert. den. 368 U.S. 930 (1961).

Geraci v. St. Xavier High School 13 Ohio Op. 3d 146 (Ohio, 1978).

Goss v. Lopez 419 U.S. 565 (1975).

LaMorte, Michael W. (1977, Fall). Rights and responsibilities in light of social contract theory. *Administration Quarterly*, 13, pp. 31-48.

Levandowski v. Jackson City School District, 328 So. 2d 339 (Minn. 1976).

National Labor Relations Board v. Catholic Bishop of Chicago, 440 U.S. 490 (1979).

New Jersey v. T.L.O. 105 S. Ct. 733 (1985).

Pastoral Statement of the Catholic Bishops on Handicapped People (1978).

Pierce v. the Society of Sisters, 268 U.S. 510 (1925).

Reardon et al. v. LeMoyne et al., 454 A. 2d 428 (N.H. 1982).

Rendell-Baker v. Kohn, 102 S. Ct. 2764 (1982).

Seavey, Warren A. (1957). Dismissal of students: due process. *Harvard Law Review* 70, 1406-1410.

Smith v. Archbishop of St. Louis, 632 S.W. 2d 516 (Mo. Ct. App. 1982).

Tinker v. Des Moines Independent Community School District et al., 393 U.S. 503 (1969).

Titus v. Lindberg, 228 A. 2d 65 (N.J., 1967).

United States Code Annotated.

United States Constitution.

Weithoff v. St. Veronica School, 210 N.W. 2d 108 (Mich. 1973).

Wisch v. Sanford School, Inc., 420 F. Supp. 1310 (1976).